Greekish

Georgina Hayden

Greek*ish*

Everyday recipes with Greek roots

BLOOMSBURY PUBLISHING
LONDON • OXFORD • NEW YORK • NEW DELHI • SYDNEY

BLOOMSBURY PUBLISHING
Bloomsbury Publishing Plc
50 Bedford Square, London, WC1B 3DP, UK
29 Earlsfort Terrace, Dublin 2, Ireland

BLOOMSBURY, BLOOMSBURY PUBLISHING and the Diana logo are trademarks of Bloomsbury Publishing Plc

First published in Great Britain 2024

A catalogue record for this book is available from the British Library
Library of Congress Cataloguing-in-Publication data has been applied for

ISBN: HB: 978-1-5266-3066-7 ; ebook: 978-1-5266-3065-0

2 4 6 8 10 9 7 5 3 1

Project editor: Holly O'Neill
Designer: Anna Green at Siulen Design
Photographer: Laura Edwards
Food stylist: Joss Herd
Prop stylist: Tabitha Hawkins
Indexer: Vanessa Bird

Printed and bound in China by Toppan Leefung Printing Ltd

To find out more about our authors and books visit www.bloomsbury.com and sign up for our newsletters.

Persephone and Elektra, my Greekish girls.

*Forever challenging me to make things
more delicious and more fun.
In the kitchen and in life.*

Contents

Introduction   10

A good start   18
Small dishes & snacks   52
  Say cheese...   62
Everyday heroes   82
  SAS: Spanakopita Appreciation Society   94
Things on sticks   132
Feasts   148
Salads, sides & vegetables   184
Sweet tooth   214
  Double negative — a mess in two parts   224
  Baklava, a love story and inspiration   242

Menus   266
Stockists   268
A glossary, and some tips on how
  to cook from this book   270
Index   276
Thank you   286

Greek*ish*...

This book? It's Greek. Ish. And if you are saying 'ish' with a scrunched-up nose, a squinted eye and a slight wobble of the head or tilt of the hand, then you are on the right track.

This is the food I like to cook every day in my Greekish life — meals that are straightforward and straight-up tasty. They nod to my Greek-Cypriot heritage, but are shaped by my busy family life. Take my simplified pastitsio (page 124); I'm always trying to find ways to make traditional but admittedly laborious dishes more quickly and my revision of the classic layered pasta bake is a triumph. Why use four pans when one will do? Hasselback imam bayildi (page 150) is an aubergine dish that I inherited from my yiayia — I've given it a fashionable name but its roots stretch back to the Ottoman Empire. Can I get my kids to eat almost anything by making it spanakopita-ish (page 96)? Spoiler: yes.

I also want to show you how I use some of my favourite Greek ingredients. I'm more likely to grate kefalotyri over pasta than parmesan (page 176); I love drizzling honey and flower waters into desserts (see almost any recipe in the Sweet Tooth chapter, page 214); and like any good Greek girl, there's always a place in my heart (and glass) for Nescafé (page 259). And we all love feta, but have you ever used it in a sweet bake (page 232)?

Until very recently, it felt like Greek food in the West was seen as basic, crude; constantly compared and found inferior to the perennially popular cuisine of its elegant neighbour, Italy. It's a thrill to see Greek and Cypriot cuisine having some time in the spotlight. The food is undeniably similar: an abundance of sun-charged vegetables, pasta and grains, and slow-cooked meats span both countries. What Greece and Cyprus also have is this heavy influence from the east. Spices, barbecues, mezedes, dips and floral sweets. This sort of food and cooking lends itself to sociable eating. I want to feed you from a table groaning with food, but I also want to chat to you (in a too-loud voice while gesticulating lots) and not be slaving away behind a stove.

When I was a child, our family holidays were always to Cyprus, to see relatives. Now I have my own children and we've been exploring mainland Greece and the islands, which has been exhilarating beyond belief. There is such diversity around the country, from the green and leafier Ionians, to effortlessly hip Thessaloniki, edgy and historical Athens and the sheer beauty of the white-washed Cyclades. My first trip to Crete blew my mind. I'd heard that rural Crete reminds Cypriots of old Cyprus, before the huge amounts of tourism, and I can see that. Staying in a sleepy village, where my daughters befriended cats and hung out in the evenings with the old boys playing cards in the *kafeneion*, surrounded by more olive trees than I had ever seen in my life, was idyllic.

The diversity inevitably extends to the food. Sure there are dishes you will be able to eat all over the country — moussaka, the classic Greek salad (horiatiki), mezedes and dips. But across the mainland and thousands of islands, the food varies greatly. I adore the heartier dishes of northern Greece, the meats slow-cooked in clay pots, tossed through handmade pasta. Syrupy filo pastries, common all over Greece and Cyprus, but in the north filled with heart-stopping amounts of cream. The use of ginger in drinks. These were less familiar to me. I devoured them all with appreciative greed and a curious mind.

The variety of foods is not only dictated by the landscape, but by neighbouring countries. To the north and east lie Albania, North Macedonia, Bulgaria and Turkey. Other culinary traditions are a legacy of the Ottoman Empire. A historical Jewish community in Thessaloniki, no longer as prevalent as it was, has left its mark. Corfu was under Venetian occupation for almost 400 years, so there is a lingering influence in the Ionians. Middle Eastern flavours emerge in the southern islands and also in Cyprus, where the similarities with the food of countries such as Syria and Lebanon are strong. And of course there are influences from both the Greek and Turkish communities on the divided island.

Continued on page 14

As a food writer, I have a constant battle between a desire to delve into foods with broader cultural roots and collective memories, versus simply writing for the sake of a good meal. It's liberating to write something just... because. Because it's what I felt like eating, because I wanted to get creative with the limitations of what I had in my cupboard. Because I wanted to get creative with no limitations. No having to cross-check sources, no crushing weight of responsibly representing my culture, no yiayia slapping my wrist telling me I'm doing it wrong. (I mean, she still did a bit; she always knows best.)

I didn't want to pigeonhole this book as 'family friendly', but that's what it is. For all families — children and partners, friends, flatmates and relatives — at all times, in groups big or small, however they fit in your life. You will find what I make when I want to cook for pleasure: low-effort, high-reward dishes so I can focus on being a vivacious host, presiding over good food and good times with my favourite people (which, you may have gathered, is my main goal in life). On the other hand, I have to cook every day for two small, unpredictable people and, honestly, sometimes it is a grind. I know the value of recipes that are easy, dependable and adaptable, and I believe all of these are.

Each recipe has been tested by and on friends, colleagues and extended family, and finally had to get approval from the most vocally opinionated critics I know: my yiayia, my dad and my girls. (Apart from salt and spice, there are very few things I won't encourage my daughters to try, and they have eaten almost everything in this book.)

Truth be told, when it comes to writing recipes, sometimes hiding behind tradition actually makes life easier. You don't like something? Take it up with my ancestors. But these Greekish dishes are all me. And I think they're some of the best I have written. I hope that you love them, that they become part of your repertoire and that over time you make them your own.

Savoury

Burnt butter eggs and goat's cheese

Ladenia smash: tomato, onion and oregano toast

Bobota: cheesy green chilli cornbread

The HLT v the HMT

Charred pepper and olive strapatsada

Village sausages, beans and peppers on toast

Breakfast soutzoukakia: meatballs in chilli tomatoes
  with eggs

Everyday yoghurt flatbreads

The toppings:

- Whipped feta with brown butter pine nuts
- Tahini, date and chocolate spread
- Salted honey butter

Sweet

Holly's baklava French toast

Pralina bougatsa: chocolate hazelnut custard filo pie

Grilled watermelon breakfast salad

Gala trin: spiced milk and pasta

Pillowy chestnut knots

Pasteli yoghurt

A good start

Burnt butter eggs and goat's cheese

In the Cretan dish staka me avga, eggs are fried in a type of clarified goat's butter (called *staka*). It is a traditional, unusual ingredient and worth hunting down if you are intrigued (see page 268 for stockists). Here I have simplified the recipe by cooking the eggs in a nutty burnt butter and finishing the dish with crumbly goat's cheese to recreate a similar flavour. A stretch perhaps, regardless it is delicious.

SERVES 2 (OR 1, IF YOU'RE ME)

1 garlic clove
25g unsalted butter
Olive oil
¼ teaspoon sweet smoked paprika
2 large eggs
Sea salt and freshly ground
 black pepper
50g goat's cheese
A few sprigs of parsley (optional)

Peel and finely slice the garlic. Put the butter in a small frying pan and place on a medium heat. Once it has melted, allow it to cook a bit further so that it starts to turn golden-brown and smell nutty. Add a drizzle of olive oil and the garlic to the pan. Cook for a minute and stir in the paprika. Crack in the eggs. Season with salt and pepper and fry for 4-5 minutes, spooning over the hot fat until the eggs are cooked through but the yolks are still a little soft (or cook more/less to your liking). Crumble the goat's cheese over the eggs. Transfer to plates, or serve in the pan, with some parsley, if you like. Perfect with any soft, fresh bread you like.

Ladenia smash:
tomato, onion and oregano toast

VG + GF

Ladenia is a rectangular olive-oil flatbread, a bit like a focaccia, from the Cycladic island of Kimlos. Traditionally a jammy tomato and onion topping is baked into the dough. I love it, but some days, especially in the morning, I don't have time to mix, knead, prove and bake bread from scratch, and I find this makes a great alternative — you're not being short-changed here. I love this most at breakfast, but also as a snack or as part of a meze. A crumbling of mizithra or feta over the top isn't essential but is, I think, always welcome.

SERVES 4

1 red onion
400g cherry tomatoes
8 garlic cloves
Olive oil
2 tablespoons pomegranate
 molasses
1 teaspoon dried oregano
Sea salt and freshly ground
 black pepper
4 slices of focaccia or ciabatta
 (gluten-free, if needed)
A few sprigs of flat-leaf parsley

Preheat your oven to 220°C/fan 200°C/gas mark 7. Peel the red onion and cut into thin wedges. Place in a roasting tray with the cherry tomatoes. Crush the garlic cloves, in their skin, with the side of your knife, add to the tray and drizzle everything liberally with olive oil. Add the pomegranate molasses, sprinkle over the dried oregano and season generously with salt and pepper. Toss everything together well, shake back out so the ingredients are in a single layer, and place in the oven. Roast for 25 minutes, until the onions are sticky and charred.

When the vegetables are ready, place a griddle pan on a high heat and char the focaccia or ciabatta slices on one side. Place them on a serving board, charred side up, and squish the garlic cloves on top, then spoon over some juices from the pan. Finely chop the parsley, stir through the vegetables, and spoon the mixture on the toasts. Serve straight away.

Bobota: *cheesy green chilli cornbread*

V + GF

Bobota isn't necessarily considered a breakfast food but is one of my favourite ways to start the day. I'll make it on a Sunday, pop it in an airtight container and the following week grab squares to have on the go. I might give it a flash in a pan or blast in the microwave for maximum cheese impact — and eating it warm means there's the option of slapping on salty butter to melt in. It is also excellent as part of a larger spread or with soup.

MAKES 9 SQUARES

Salted butter, for the tin and
 to serve
1 bunch of spring onions
1–2 green chillies, to taste
200g fine cornmeal
200g plain flour (gluten-free,
 if needed)
1 teaspoon baking powder
½ teaspoon bicarbonate of soda
1 teaspoon sea salt
200g Greek yoghurt
3 tablespoons honey
2 large eggs
225ml whole milk
130ml olive oil
200g feta
150g cheddar

Preheat your oven to 200°C/180°C fan/gas mark 6. Butter and line a 23cm square cake tin with greaseproof paper. Trim and finely slice the spring onions. Halve, deseed and finely slice the chillies. In a large mixing bowl, whisk the spring onions and chillies together with the cornmeal, plain flour, baking powder, bicarbonate of soda and sea salt. Create a well in the middle of the dry ingredients and spoon in the Greek yoghurt, honey and eggs. Whisk them in till just combined, then use a large metal spoon to slowly fold in the milk and olive oil. Crumble in three-quarters of the feta. Cut the cheddar into small pieces and fold in most of it.

Spoon the mixture into the prepared tin, scatter over the remaining cheeses and bake for 30-35 minutes, until golden and cooked through. When a skewer inserted in the centre comes out clean, apart from any gooey cheese, it's done. Cool in the tin for 10 minutes, then transfer to a rack and leave to cool — if you can. It's best served warm with a knob of butter on top oozing in, but if you want it for breakfasts later, leave it to cool down completely before cutting and storing.

The HLT v the HMT

V + GF

Lountza is probably the most popular cured meat in Cyprus. Pork loin is marinated in red wine and spices such as coriander seeds and cumin, before being smoked. It is lean, and is often eaten finely sliced or grilled in a sandwich — usually with halloumi. If you've been to Cyprus I'll bet good money that you've indulged in a halloumi-lountza-tomato *santouits*. It's a classic, a staple, a craving... My version includes a spread of apricot jam, because it's my all-time favourite halloumi accessory. I've also given you an option for using mushroom instead of lountza. Those who don't eat meat needn't miss out, and it is just as good.

SERVES 1

1 submarine roll or 2 slices of
 fresh white bread (gluten-free,
 if needed)
Salted butter, at room
 temperature
1 tablespoon apricot jam
2 tablespoons mayonnaise
1 ripe tomato
A few slices of cucumber
75g halloumi
2 slices of lountza or back bacon
 or 1 large portobello mushroom
Olive oil
A pinch of dried oregano

Cut open your submarine roll, or lay out your two slices of bread, on a chopping board or plate. Butter one side, then spread with the apricot jam. Spread the other with the mayonnaise. Slice the tomato, and place on top of the mayo with the cucumber. Slice the halloumi into three. If using, slice the mushroom into 1cm slices.

Place a large frying pan on a medium heat and add a drizzle of olive oil. Depending on which you are using, fry the lountza, bacon or portobello mushroom slices until slightly golden, then sprinkle a pinch of oregano over the top. The lountza won't take long as it's already cooked; it just needs a bit of colour. The bacon will need a few minutes, or cook it how you like it. The mushroom slices will need 2–3 minutes on each side, on a higher heat. When your protein is done, push to one side of the pan and fry the halloumi slices on both sides, until golden-crusted.

Place the lountza/bacon/mushroom on top of the cucumber, add the halloumi and top with the apricot-spread bread. Squish down, cut in half and go for it.

Charred pepper and olive strapatsada

This is an amalgamation of a few delicious things: Cypriot ntomatas me avga (tomatoes and eggs), more commonly known in Greece as strapatsada; Turkish menemen (essentially the same thing but with peppers); and my dad's favourite breakfast, grilled olives. If you've never tried barbecuing olives, it's such a great thing to do; it makes them meatier and even more intense. (If you're curious, soak a bamboo skewer, or use a fine metal skewer, and thread on black olives, then grill for a few minutes each side. You can also dry-fry or grill them in a pan, as I have here.) Dad loves the wrinkly black ones, charred then crushed on toast with extra virgin olive oil, and I've used their punchy flavour to finish my eggs. You can use any peppers you have, but I prefer at least one red for a bit of sweetness.

SERVES 4

2 peppers, at least 1 red one
50g stoned black olives, ideally
   the wrinkly ones but kalamata
   are fine
1 red onion
Olive oil
3 ripe tomatoes
1 heaped tablespoon tomato purée
   (sun-dried tomato purée would
   be great here if you have it)
1 teaspoon caster sugar
1 teaspoon Aleppo pepper (or
   ½ teaspoon dried red chilli flakes)
1 teaspoon dried oregano
Sea salt and freshly ground
   black pepper
6 large eggs

V, DF
+ GF

Place a griddle pan on a high heat. Quarter the peppers, remove and discard the stalks and seeds, and place the peppers skin-side down on the hot griddle. Alternatively, you can do this in a frying pan. Whichever you choose, the pan needs to be dry, without oil. Add the olives, too, and leave everything for 8–10 minutes, until they start to char (turn the olives after 5 minutes). Meanwhile, peel and finely chop the red onion.

Place three tablespoons of olive oil in a large frying pan and pop on a medium-low heat. Add the red onion and let it start to sauté. Remove the peppers and olives from the griddle and leave to cool slightly. Finely chop the tomatoes and add to the onions along with the tomato purée, caster sugar, Aleppo pepper, dried oregano and a generous pinch each of salt and pepper. Give it a stir, and continue to sauté while you chop the peppers into 1–2cm pieces. Add them to the pan, turn the heat up a little and cook everything together for 10 minutes, stirring more frequently towards the end, until thickened and rich.

Whisk the eggs with a pinch each of salt and pepper. Push the pepper mixture to one side of the pan, slide your pan off the heat, reduce the heat to low and pour the whisked eggs into the pan. Gently ripple everything together and return the pan to the heat. Cook for 3 minutes, stirring once or twice, until the eggs are just cooked and set. Chop the olives and scatter over the top before serving.

Village sausages, beans and peppers on toast

This recipe started out as a one-pot dinner for my kids. I had my heart set on making fasolia (Greek bean stew) and ended up with this. Once I was done I decided to serve it on toast, and it reminded me of tinned beans with sausage in them. I mean that in the best possible way! It was my childhood all over again, and it went down a storm with my girls. I make it often now, and it's become one of our favourite lazy weekend brunches. Make it for whichever meal you like, just make sure you have it with toast or nice bread — maybe a grating of cheese, if you want to go all out.

SERVES 4

Olive oil
400g sausages (about 6) — if
  you can get ones laced with
  a little chilli or fennel, they will
  work nicely
1 red onion
2 garlic cloves
3 red, orange or yellow peppers
1 teaspoon dried oregano
2 tablespoons tomato purée
¾ teaspoon sweet smoked paprika
1 × 400g tin of white beans (white
  kidney, borlotti or cannellini — all
  are good)
1 bay leaf
250ml beef or chicken stock
Sea salt and freshly ground
  black pepper
Toast or bread, to serve
  (gluten-free, if needed)

Place a large ovenproof saucepan or cast-iron skillet on a medium heat. Pour in a layer of olive oil. Squeeze the sausage meat out of the skins into little meatballs, and fry for 8-10 minutes, until browned all over. While they are cooking, prepare the vegetables. Peel and finely chop the red onion and garlic. Halve, deseed and slice the peppers into 1cm strips.

When the sausage meatballs are ready, add all the chopped vegetables to the pan along with the dried oregano and fry for 5 minutes. Stir in the tomato purée and sweet smoked paprika, then add the tinned beans, including the liquid. Stir in the bay leaf and stock and bring everything to the boil. Season well, cover with a lid, reduce the heat a little and simmer for 30 minutes.

When the beans are almost ready, preheat your grill to high. Place the pan under the grill and grill for 5-8 minutes, until the top is crisping up and turning golden-brown. Serve spoonfuls on top of buttery toast, or with fresh crusty bread.

GF + DF

Breakfast soutzoukakia:
meatballs in chilli tomatoes with eggs

GF + DF

This is a versatile dish. It makes a lovely family dinner but is perhaps most perfect for a hangover-busting brunch. If I'm making it for littles, or someone not so keen on spice, I'll halve the amount of cumin and add the chilli at the end to individual portions. Play with the spices and make the recipe your own, depending on your own taste. It's delicious with pita and maybe a side of pickles or olives, too.

SERVES 4

500g beef mince
½ teaspoon ground cinnamon
2 teaspoons sweet smoked
 paprika
2 teaspoons ground cumin
Sea salt and freshly ground
 black pepper
½ bunch of coriander
2 tablespoons olive oil, plus a little
 extra, if needed
2 onions
2 garlic cloves
2 red chillies
2 × 400g tins of plum tomatoes
1 tablespoon red wine vinegar,
 plus a little extra, if needed
4 large eggs

Place the mince in a mixing bowl and add the cinnamon and ½ teaspoon each of the paprika and cumin and season well. Finely chop the coriander leaves and add half (keep the stalks). Knead or squish the mix together well to combine, then roll heaped teaspoons into balls. If you wet your hands occasionally, the mix won't stick to them as much. Place a large frying pan on a medium heat and add two tablespoons of olive oil. Fry the meatballs for 8–10 minutes, turning, until just browned all over. You might need to do this in batches, so as not to overcrowd the pan; place the cooked ones on a plate as you go.

Meanwhile, peel and finely chop the onions and garlic and finely slice the chillies (remove the seeds if you don't want it too spicy). Finely slice the reserved coriander stalks. Remove the meatballs from the pan and keep aside on a plate, if you haven't already. You want two tablespoons of oil in the pan, so add a little more if needed. Add all the chopped vegetables to the pan and sauté for 10 minutes. Stir in the remaining paprika and cumin. Fry for a minute then add the tinned tomatoes, breaking them up with a wooden spoon, then add the red wine vinegar. Season well, bring to the boil, then reduce the heat and simmer for 10 minutes, stirring occasionally to further break up the tomatoes.

Taste the sauce and adjust for seasoning and vinegar as needed. Carefully add the meatballs back to the pan and cook for a further 5 minutes. Make four wells in the sauce and crack an egg into each one. Season well, reduce the heat a little and cover with a lid. Cook for 3 minutes, until the eggs are just cooked; have a look and cook for a little longer if needed or you like them well done. Scatter with the remaining coriander leaves and serve.

Everyday yoghurt flatbreads

This is a recipe that still feels magical to me. I understand how it happens but turning just two ingredients into fluffy, charred bread... It's the kind of science that makes me happy. I've seen some recipes that are overcomplicated with yeast and other ingredients; trust me, it's not necessary. If you haven't ever made them, please, please give them a go — they really are easy enough to make first thing for breakfast. Also, I'm happy to say I sometimes make this recipe with dairy-free yoghurt for a vegan version and it works a treat.

MAKES 4–8, SERVES 4

250g self-raising flour
250g Greek yoghurt (plant-based, if needed)
Olive oil
½ teaspoon sea salt

Place the self-raising flour in a large bowl and mix in the yoghurt, 1 tablespoon of olive oil and the sea salt. Stir with a fork until it all comes together, then knead with your hands until you have a smooth dough. Evenly divide the dough into four to eight pieces, depending on how large you want your flatbreads. Roll into balls and then roll out each into a circle, 1cm thick. Place a large frying pan on a medium heat. Drizzle in a little olive oil and add a flatbread. Cover with a lid, cook for 1 minute, then remove the lid and cook for another minute. Flip it over and cook for a further 2–3 minutes uncovered. Remove from the pan and wrap in a tea towel to keep warm while you fry the remaining flatbreads, adding a drizzle of extra oil as needed. When they're all cooked, serve the flatbreads immediately.

For flatbread toppings, see page 38

Clockwise from top left: everyday yoghurt flatbreads (page 34); tahini, date and chocolate spread (page 39); whipped feta with brown butter pine nuts (page 38); salted honey butter (page 39)

Everyday yoghurt flatbread toppings

V + GF

Whipped feta with brown butter pine nuts

Whipped feta is a great addition to your repertoire. As a dip? Gorgeous. Part of a feast with grilled meat, seafood or vegetables? Yes please. Next to fruit salad, drizzled with honey? An elegant breakfast. I've topped it here with a pine nut and chilli butter, for a rich, spicy finish. Make sure you cook enough flatbreads, because everyone will fight over this.

SERVES 6

200g feta
200g Greek yoghurt
½ lemon
Sea salt and freshly ground
 black pepper
2 green chillies
½ bunch of oregano or thyme
25g unsalted butter
2 tablespoons olive oil
20g pine nuts

Crumble the feta into a mixing bowl. Stir in the Greek yoghurt and squeeze in the lemon juice. Season well. Use a stick blender to blitz it all until just smooth. Do not over-blitz this or it'll end up runny, and don't be tempted to do this in a high-speed blender, because it will liquidise. If it does become a little runny, pop the mixture into a serving bowl and place in the fridge to firm up (taste it and adjust the seasoning at this point).

When you are ready to eat, halve, deseed and finely slice the chillies. Pick the herb leaves from the stems. Place the butter in a small saucepan with the olive oil. Stir in the pine nuts and the herb leaves. Heat over a medium-low heat. By the time the pine nuts are golden, the butter will be nutty and golden-brown. Remove the pan from the heat and stir in the sliced chillies. Spoon the whipped feta on a plate or in a bowl, make a shallow well in the top, pour over the spiced pine nut butter and serve.

Tahini, date and chocolate spread

VG + GF

Cypriots, like most people from the Middle East, use tahini in both savoury and sweet recipes. Here, its earthy, nutty qualities combine so well with bitter chocolate and caramel-sweet dates, not to mention the texture they bring, and create something special. For such a simple recipe, it is a surprisingly complex mouthful.

SERVES 10-12

75g dark chocolate, 70% cocoa
125g tahini
90g medjool dates
¼ teaspoon flaky sea salt

Break the chocolate into even pieces, and melt in a microwave or in a heatproof bowl set over a pan of simmering water. Stir the melted chocolate until smooth. In a blender or food processor, mix the tahini with 75ml of boiling water. Stone the dates, then add to the tahini mix and blitz until smooth, adding a splash more boiling water if it is too thick. Fold through the molten chocolate and sea salt. Mix until smooth, then decant to a sterilised jar and leave to cool and firm up. Don't worry about storing in the fridge; as long as the jar is sterilised it will be happy enough at room temperature. It won't hang around for long!

Salted honey butter

V + GF

A few years ago I hosted a charity supper club and the most popular dish was my grilled halloumi (see page 68), but instead of using apricots, I basted it with a salted honey butter that had been donated to us. This is my homage. Slap it on yoghurt flatbread, fried halloumi, in a ham sandwich (trust me) — whatever floats your boat.

MAKES ABOUT 200G

100g unsalted butter, at room
  temperature
6-7 tablespoons honey, plus extra
  to serve
¼ teaspoon ground cinnamon
½ teaspoon flaky sea salt, plus
  extra to serve
A few sprigs of thyme (optional)

Place the butter, six tablespoons of honey and the cinnamon in a mixing bowl, or the bowl of a stand mixer. Add ¼ teaspoon of the sea salt. Beat with an electric mixer for 5-7 minutes, until creamy, light and whipped. Have a taste, then beat in more salt and/or honey as you like. Transfer to an airtight container. However I use this, I like to finish the dish with a drizzle of honey, a pinch of flaky sea salt and a few sprigs of thyme on top.

Holly's baklava French toast

V + GF

I inherited this recipe from my good friend Holly, who has an appreciation of not only Greek food but also brunch — they do it so well, Australians. If you have a sweet tooth in the morning, this is the one for you. It takes the flavours of baklava but swaps the crisp filo for soft brioche — the syrupy goodness remains. This also makes a delicious dessert, and you could layer up the elements in a dish to bake it bread and butter pudding style. For a more extensive appreciation of the flavours of baklava, head to page 242.

SERVES 4

1 orange
3 tablespoons honey
2 teaspoons orange blossom
  water (optional)
70g walnuts, plus extra, chopped,
  to serve
2 tablespoons caster sugar,
  plus a couple of extra pinches
  for the soaking mixture and
  for frying
¼ teaspoon ground cinnamon, plus
  a pinch extra
60g salted butter, room
  temperature
6 slices brioche (gluten-free,
  if needed)
2 large eggs
100ml whole milk
A pinch of sea salt
Greek yoghurt or labneh, to serve

Zest a few scrapes of the orange peel finely into a shallow bowl and set aside. Squeeze the orange juice into a small pan with the honey and orange blossom water and bring to the boil. Leave to bubble away for 2–3 minutes until syrupy. Leave to one side. Chop the walnuts into a rubble of medium-fine pieces. Put a frying pan on a medium heat and add the walnuts and start to toast. Add in the caster sugar. Stir to coat the nuts in the sugar, then add the ground cinnamon. Continue toasting briefly until everything smells wonderful — do not let it burn. Transfer to a plate and leave to cool.

Spread 50g of the butter across the six slices of brioche. Sprinkle about a quarter of the nuts over one slice of brioche. Top with another slice, butter side up, and sprinkle over a further quarter of nuts, then top with a final slice, butter-side down. Repeat with the remaining nuts and brioche. Cut each layered sandwich in half diagonally. In the shallow bowl with the orange zest, whisk the eggs and milk until smooth, and then whisk in a pinch each of salt, sugar and cinnamon. Place the sandwiches in the egg mixture; soak for 3 minutes, then flip and soak for a further 3 minutes.

Place half the remaining butter in a frying pan and fry the sandwiches for 2–3 minutes, until lightly golden, then flip over and repeat. Add the extra butter to the pan if needed during cooking. When they're almost ready, sprinkle the bread with a little caster sugar, flip over and cook for a further minute on all sides until caramelised and a little crunchy. Serve with the orange honey and a sprinkling of more chopped walnuts, if you like. Dreamy with a dollop of Greek yoghurt or labneh.

Pralina bougatsa:
chocolate hazelnut custard filo pie

Bougatsa, a type of filo pie, is a popular breakfast all over Greece. The classic version is filled with a semolina custard. In bakeries, trays of it are dusted with icing sugar by the heavy hand of an efficient server who hacks up bougatsa all day. I have given a sheet quantity for the filo pastry, as that's what's important, rather than a weight. If possible, seek out a good Greek or Middle Eastern brand. The filo you get from large supermarkets is thicker and not as pliable. A more authentic brand will make all the difference.

MAKES 6

100g hazelnuts
125g light soft brown sugar
90g fine semolina
3 large eggs
2 teaspoons vanilla extract,
 or paste if you have it
500ml whole milk
About 100ml double cream
125g unsalted butter
12 sheets of filo (405g) — you need
 them to be about 48cm × 25cm,
 so if yours are much bigger, use 6
6 tablespoons good-quality
 chocolate hazelnut spread
3 tablespoons icing sugar
1 teaspoon ground cinnamon
 (optional)

Preheat your oven to 200°C/180°C fan/gas mark 6. Place 60g of the hazelnuts in a small baking dish and pop in the oven for 7–8 minutes to toast lightly. Leave to one side to cool.

In a large mixing bowl, whisk together the brown sugar, fine semolina, eggs and vanilla extract. Place the milk in a large saucepan on a medium heat and when it is warm but not boiling, ladle a few spoonfuls into the egg mixture, whisking in straight away until smooth. Pour the egg mixture back into the pan and cook for 3–4 minutes, whisking constantly, until smooth and significantly thickened. Remove from the heat. Leave to cool for 15 minutes, but whisk occasionally to stop a skin forming. It will thicken even more, so gradually add some double cream to thin it a little. You might not need the whole amount, but keep whisking until you have a thick, spoonable custard.

Melt the butter and use it to grease a baking sheet. Chop both the toasted and untoasted hazelnuts, keeping them separate. Take a sheet of filo out, and have the short edge facing you. Brush with butter all over and top with a second sheet, or fold in half if you're using large sheets. Butter again. Towards the bottom of the sheet, in the centre, add a spoonful of chocolate spread. Top with a sixth of the toasted nuts, then five tablespoons of the custard. Roll the pastry up once, away from you, then tuck in both sides and keep rolling until you have a large parcel. Place on the tray and repeat with the rest of the ingredients, so you have six filo parcels. Brush all the bougatsas with the remaining butter and scatter with the untoasted hazelnuts. Bake for 25–30 minutes, until dark golden all over. Dust liberally with icing sugar and ground cinnamon, if you like. Leave for 10 minutes before serving.

Grilled watermelon breakfast salad

V + GF

Watermelon is the best summer breakfast, and here's a recipe for when you want to be a bit fancy with it. Grilling watermelon is always a great idea: it becomes dense, more intense in flavour and caramelised — heavenly in sweet or savoury dishes. Make this when you want to eat it; don't leave it to sit around as the melon becomes watery. If you're not into the idea of grilled watermelon (no judgement, I know hot melon is not for everyone), then make this with fresh watermelon chunks. It'll still be excellent.

SERVES 4

1kg watermelon
2 tablespoons sesame seeds,
 a mix of white and black will
 be nice
1 teaspoon nigella seeds
150g feta
100g Greek yoghurt
4 sprigs of mint
70g pistachios
2–3 tablespoons honey

Cut away the watermelon rind, then cut the flesh into cubes of about 3cm. In a large frying pan on a medium-high heat, toast the sesame and nigella seeds until the sesame seeds are pale golden and everything is fragrant. Remove from the pan to a bowl and leave them to cool. Mix the feta with the yoghurt until just smooth. I do this with a stick blender, but do not over-mix, or it will go thin and liquidy. Stir in the cooled seeds, then spread on a platter. Pick the leaves from the mint sprigs and finely shred with a knife. Sprinkle a third over the feta-yoghurt. Roughly chop the pistachios and keep to one side.

Place the large frying pan back on a medium heat. You can also use a griddle. Fry the watermelon, in batches if needed, for 4 minutes on one side, till it looks softened but toasted on the underside. Drizzle with one or two tablespoons of honey, turn once and fry for another 4 minutes. Because of the honey, this side may char a little more.

Place the melon on the feta-yoghurt spread, and drizzle over any juices from the pan and more honey to taste. Scatter over the pistachios and remaining mint and serve immediately.

Gala trin: *spiced milk and pasta*

My second book, *Taverna*, featured the recipe for fide me to gala: vermicelli cooked in milk. It is very traditional, comforting and sweet, and my mum's favourite breakfast. She loves it in the same way that some people love porridge. Sometimes she makes it with broken tagliatelle, and then it's known as gala trin. I can't help but embellish tradition by adding a few of my favourite aromatic spices. Use only tagliatelle, sugar and milk and you'll have my mum's version.

SERVES 2

25g unsalted butter (dairy-free, if needed)
50g dried tagliatelle (gluten-free, if needed)
2 tablespoons caster sugar
700ml milk (whole milk, or use a plant-based option)
2 cardamom pods
½ stick of cinnamon

Place the butter in a medium-sized saucepan on a medium-low heat. Melt the butter and let it turn deep golden-brown and nutty; this will take about 5 minutes. Meanwhile, break up the tagliatelle so it is in bite-sized lengths. Stir the pasta into the butter along with the sugar and leave it for a couple of minutes, letting it all caramelise slightly. Stir in the milk. Crush the cardamom pods and add to the pan with the cinnamon stick and bring to the boil. Once the milk is boiling, reduce the heat and leave the pasta to cook for 20-25 minutes, stirring occasionally, until tender. Remove the pan from the heat and leave to cool slightly before serving, for about 5 minutes, so it has a chance to thicken and become creamy.

Pillowy chestnut knots

You'll often find chestnut sellers in cities around Greece and Cyprus; the smell from the pans over an open flame strikes a deeply nostalgic note for me. I grew up eating chestnuts roasted like this but as an adult I had them in little pillowy buns in Thessaloniki. They were glorious. This is the sort of sweet breakfast that wins me over: freshly baked bread, with a sugary crust that you can't help but lick your lips for.

MAKES 12 BUNS

250ml whole milk
1 × 7g sachet of fast-action yeast
120g caster sugar
500g strong white bread flour
1½ teaspoons mixed spice
1½ teaspoons fine sea salt
140g unsalted butter, at room temperature
1 large egg
Olive oil
150g light soft brown sugar
2 teaspoons vanilla extract
200g chestnut purée

Warm the milk, so it is still comfortable to touch, and mix in the yeast and one tablespoon of the caster sugar and set aside for a few minutes. Place the flour in a large mixing bowl, or the bowl of a stand mixer, and mix in the mixed spice and one teaspoon of the fine sea salt. Melt 40g of the butter and pour into the flour. Crack in the egg and pour in the yeast mixture. Knead for 8-10 minutes, until you have a smooth, elastic dough. Clean out the bowl, drizzle with olive oil and pop the dough back in. Leave somewhere warm to rise for 1-2 hours, or until doubled in size.

Beat the remaining 100g of butter and ½ teaspoon of salt with the brown sugar and vanilla. Mix in the chestnut purée. Turn out the dough on a lightly floured surface, gently knock out the air and roll out in a rectangle, about 50cm × 40cm, with the longer edge facing you. Spread the chestnut mixture over the top two-thirds of the dough. Fold the unbuttered third in towards the middle, then fold over the top third. Gently roll the dough with a rolling pin to flatten it a little; you'll end up with a long thin rectangle.

Trim the ends then cut the dough into 12 equal strips. How you twist your knots is up to you; there are many techniques. I like to cut the rectangle in half lengthways from the bottom, so it is still connected at the top, then twist the strips together. I then knot the twisted dough, press in the seams and place on a baking sheet. You'll find a lot of the butter will come out when making the knots; scoop it up and spread it back over the dough. Prove the knotted buns for 45 minutes, or overnight in the fridge.

Preheat your oven to 200°C/180°C fan/gas mark 6. Bake the buns for 18-20 minutes, until deep golden. Place the remaining caster sugar into a mixing bowl, so that when the buns are still hot you can toss them through for a sugar coating. Leave on a rack to cool before eating.

(Photos overleaf)

V

Pasteli yoghurt

Pasteli, a sesame brittle that's hard to stop eating, is a popular snack found throughout Greece and Cyprus. There are many variations of seeds and nuts used, and I like them all. I really love this slightly softer version crumbled over the tangiest Greek yoghurt I can find. It's a great breakfast, but also makes an elegant dessert — just add seasonal fruit.

SERVES 10-12

100g walnuts
50g unsalted butter
8 tablespoons honey, plus extra
  to serve
100g caster sugar
1 teaspoon ground cinnamon
60g sesame seeds
50g pumpkin seeds
¾ teaspoon sea salt
Greek yoghurt and fresh fruit,
  to serve

Line a large baking tray with greaseproof paper. Roughly chop the walnuts. Place the butter in a small saucepan with the honey and caster sugar and melt together. Stir in the ground cinnamon, sesame seeds, chopped walnuts, pumpkin seeds and sea salt. Keep stirring until everything is coated well, then allow to bubble away for 8-10 minutes, stirring occasionally, until everything darkens in colour and starts smelling like toffee. Remove from the heat. Quickly spread out over the lined baking tray and leave to cool completely.

Break or bash the pasteli into small pieces, a mixture of textures is nice, and scatter over Greek yoghurt. Serve as is or with fruit and a drizzle of honey. Store any leftover pasteli in an airtight container.

Snacks

Chickpea and herb keftedes
Riganada tart with anchovies
Spiced honey calamari
A beer with a side of battered gigantes

Say cheese

Filo-wrapped feta with spiced honey
Fried sesame cheese bites
Whole grilled halloumi with apricots
Figs and dates with anari and rosemary
A jar of marinated feta, a suggestion

Dips

Beetroot and dill tzatziki with fried capers
Sizzling melitzanosalata: aubergine salad/dip
Artichoke houmous
Herby skordalia: garlic dip
Everything pita chips

Small dishes & snacks

Chickpea and herb keftedes

VG + GF

Greeks and Cypriots love keftedes. These are meatballs or fritters made with whatever is good or in season — pork ones in Cyprus, tomato ones from Santorini — and one of my favourites is revithokeftedes, made with chickpeas. Naturally, they're quite like falafel, as it's the same process of soaking and blitzing uncooked chickpeas. But in Greek fashion there is potato in there, which changes the texture. Texture is key here: you need to blitz the mixture enough that it's easily shaped into fritters stable enough to fry, but you don't want it to be so smooth that there's no bite. Get it right and you'll have a snack that's utterly delicious and irresistibly moreish. You will need to start this recipe a day ahead.

SERVES 4–6

125g dried chickpeas
1 teaspoon bicarbonate of soda
200g waxy potatoes
1 onion
½ bunch of mixed soft herbs,
  whatever is in your fridge and
  needs using— flat-leaf parsley,
  mint, dill and coriander are
  all good
Sea salt and freshly ground
  black pepper
50g plain flour (gluten-free,
  if needed)
Olive oil
1 lemon

You'll need to soak the chickpeas the night before you want to make the keftedes. Place them in a large bowl with the bicarbonate of soda and cover with lots of cold water and leave overnight.

When you are ready to make the keftedes, roughly chop the potatoes (leave the skin on) and place in a small pan of water. Bring to the boil then cook for 10 minutes, or until tender. Drain and leave to steam-dry and cool.

While the potatoes cool, peel and chop the onion. Roughly chop the herbs. Drain the soaked chickpeas well, and place in a food processor with the herbs, cooled potatoes and chopped onion. Season with salt and pepper. Pulse for a minute, then blitz until it just comes together. You don't want it totally smooth or like a purée; try to keep a bit of texture in there. Remove the blade from the bowl, add the flour and stir to combine. When you're ready to fry the mixture, place a large frying pan on a medium heat and pour in enough olive oil to cover the base by 1cm. With wet hands, scoop up about a tablespoon of the mixture and roll into a ball, then flatten it slightly. Place on a clean plate until all the mixture is used up. Line a plate with kitchen paper.

Fry the fritters in batches for 3–4 minutes on each side, until deep golden, pressing them down slightly with the back of a fish slice. When they're cooked, transfer to the paper-lined plate and keep going until you've cooked all the keftedes. Serve with an extra sprinkle of salt to serve and the lemon cut into wedges, ready for squeezing over.

Riganada tart with anchovies

Riganada is a popular Kefalonian snack, and you'll find variations of it across Greece — it's not dissimilar to the more well-known dakos from Crete. It is usually a piece of stale bread, toast or a rusk that is topped with seasoned tomatoes and a variety of extras including capers, olives, sardines or feta. It will always have lots of oregano, for which the Greek work is *rigani*, hence the name. This tart is my riff on this dish. I like to prepare it ahead of having people round. It's simple and meditative to make (lining up those tomato rows) and it is exactly the kind of thing I want to snack on when having a drink — satisfyingly salty.

SERVES 8 AS A SNACK

400g ripe vine tomatoes
Sea salt and freshly ground
 black pepper
1 red onion
500g puff pastry
1 large egg
30g anchovies or sardines, in
 oil (or capers for a vegetarian
 version)
1 teaspoon dried oregano
Olive oil (optional)
A few sprigs of oregano or basil

Preheat the oven to 210°C/190°C fan/gas mark 6½ and line a baking sheet with greaseproof paper. Finely slice the tomatoes with a sharp knife (I find a small serrated knife is best), so they are less than 5mm thick. Place in a large colander and toss the tomato slices with ½ teaspoon of sea salt. Leave the colander in the sink. Peel and finely slice the red onion. Roll the puff pastry into a rectangle, about 32cm × 25cm, and score a border 2cm from the edge. Transfer to the lined baking sheet.

Whisk the egg with a splash of water and brush the border of the pastry twice. Lay three or four rows of the sliced tomatoes inside the pastry border, nestling in slices of onion as you go. When it's all done, lay on the anchovies or capers. Sprinkle over the dried oregano and drizzle with two tablespoons of the oil from the anchovy tin or jar (or use olive oil).

Pop the tray in the oven for 25–30 minutes, until the border is golden all over and nicely risen. Leave the tart to cool, then tear over the oregano or basil leaves and cut into thin slices. Serve at aperitivo time — basically, this is really nice with a glass of something very cold and a bit fizzy.

Spiced honey calamari

Sitting by the Aegean (or Mediterranean, or Ionian) Sea with oregano-sprinkled chips, crisp calamari and a cold rosé or beer has to be one of life's greatest pleasures. When I make calamari at home, I love to ramp up the flavours in the coating, and adding a bit of sweetness to finish works so well.

SERVES 4

500g squid, or calamari rings
200ml whole milk
1 teaspoon fine sea salt
150g plain flour (gluten-free, if needed)
50g cornflour
½ teaspoon baking powder
1½ teaspoons dried oregano
1 teaspoon sweet smoked paprika, plus extra to finish
1 teaspoon freshly ground black pepper
1 litre of vegetable oil, for deep-frying
2 tablespoons honey
Flaky sea salt, to finish
2 lemons

If you're using squid tubes, give them a rinse and pat dry, and then slice into 1.5-2cm rings. Place in a mixing bowl and stir in the milk and ½ teaspoon of sea salt. Cover and leave in the fridge for at least 20 minutes. In a large mixing bowl, whisk together the plain flour, cornflour, baking powder, dried oregano, paprika, ground black pepper and remaining ½ teaspoon of sea salt. Drain the squid and toss it through the flour mixture until well coated.

Pour the vegetable oil in a wide saucepan and place on a medium heat. Place one small piece of calamari in the pan, and when it starts to vigorously sizzle and turn golden, you know the oil is ready. Line a plate with kitchen paper and start to fry the calamari in batches; you don't want to overcrowd the pan. Fry for 5-6 minutes, until deep golden, then transfer to the kitchen paper-lined plate for a minute to drain. Keep going until all the calamari has been fried. Serve as you go with a drizzle of honey, pinches of flaky sea salt and sweet smoked paprika, and lemon wedges on the side for squeezing over.

A beer with a side of battered gigantes

VG + GF

This is more involved than serving up dishes of ready-made salty dried broad beans and nuts, but these fried beans are fun and addictive and take just two minutes to cook. This makes quite a lot. You can definitely halve this recipe and it will still work a treat, but once you start frying you might as well keep going and be the host who makes the best snacks — an accolade I seriously strive for.

SERVES 6-8

500ml vegetable oil, for
 deep-frying
2 × 400g tins of butter beans
100g self-raising flour
 (gluten-free, if needed)
2 teaspoons sweet
 smoked paprika
1½ teaspoons dried oregano, plus
 extra to serve
1½ teaspoons garlic granules
Sea salt and freshly ground
 black pepper
About 200ml sparkling water

Pour the oil in a medium-sized pan and place on a medium heat. Heat the oil to 180°C. Alternatively, place a cube of bread in the oil; when it turns golden-brown, the oil is ready. While the oil is heating, drain the butter beans and dry them on kitchen paper. Toss them with one tablespoon of the flour to further dry the surface.

In a large mixing bowl, whisk together the remaining self-raising flour, sweet smoked paprika, dried oregano, garlic granules and season generously with two teaspoons of salt and some black pepper. Gradually whisk in enough sparkling water until you have a smooth batter that is the same viscosity as thick double cream — start with 170ml and go from there. Stir in the dried butter beans. Line a plate with kitchen paper.

When the oil is ready, use a slotted spoon to spoon in some of the beans and fry for 2 minutes, until golden and crisp. Do not be tempted to fry too many at once or cook for longer, or they'll go mushy and also maybe explode. Drain, and transfer to the paper-lined plate to absorb the excess oil. Repeat with the remaining beans — depending on the size of your pan, you want to do it in up to four batches. Serve with extra salt and dried oregano sprinkled on top, and a glass of cold, cold beer.

Say cheese...

What did the cheese say when it looked in the mirror?

I'm a grown woman, but I love a cheese joke. I love cheese full stop. There is more halloumi in my fridge than any other food stuff. My taste buds and stomach must know it's in my lineage, part of my blood, my roots. If there is ever a day where I don't have all the ingredients to knock up a halloumi and apricot jam sandwich then you'll know things are not OK.

Greece and Cyprus aren't regarded for their cheeses in the same way as the UK, France and Italy, but they can claim a couple of big hitters. People swoon over halloumi, and that's not (only) me being patriotic. The whole salt-fat-melty-dense experience hits all the right buttons. It's also more versatile than you might think. The same goes for feta — it may not be as hardy as halloumi, but wrap it in filo and fry it (page 64) and you have a thing of crisp-then-squidgy beauty. Less known are graviera (semi-hard and similar to gruyère) and kefalotyri (hard, salty and good for grating), Greek cheeses also made with goat's and sheep's milk, although graviera is likely to have cow's milk in the mix, too. They're nuttier and tangier than, say, cheddar, with excellent melting quality, essential for deep-frying (page 67). Then, there's kefalograviera (a combination of both), versatile kaseri, mild and creamy manouri, and mizithra or Cypriot anari (both like ricotta, in fresh or salted and dried versions) — it's worth getting to know all the Greek cheeses you can find.

Oh, and the answer to the joke — and everything, really — is halloumi. *Hallou-mi!*

Filo-wrapped feta with spiced honey

The energy you'll use to make this recipe compared to the pleasure you'll get from eating it are not equal. It is the easiest thing to prepare and will pretty much guarantee you a standing ovation as you present it to the table. If you don't get at least one gasp then you are cooking for the wrong people. Get new friends, trade in your family.

Some recipes can take any old filo, but this one works best with the thin kind that you'll find in Greek or Turkish supermarkets. Hunt some down — it will be worth it.

MAKES 1 PARCEL, TO SERVE 2 AS A STARTER OR 4 AS PART OF A MEZE

1 × 200g block of feta
1 sheet of filo
Olive or vegetable oil
Sea salt and freshly ground
 black pepper
1 garlic clove
2 tablespoons honey
1 teaspoon wine vinegar, red
 or white
½ teaspoon Aleppo pepper (or
 ¼ teaspoon dried red chilli flakes)
5 sprigs of thyme

Wrap the feta in kitchen paper and set aside to dry out a little, patting away the excess moisture. Lay out the sheet of filo, brush with the oil, and season well. Pat dry the feta, then place on the filo's short edge and roll it up, folding in the edges before the last fold. Crush the garlic with the side of your knife and place in a small bowl with the honey, vinegar and one tablespoon of water. Add half the Aleppo pepper and pick in half of the thyme leaves.

Drizzle a couple of tablespoons of oil into the base of a small frying pan, and fry the parcel on a medium heat until golden-brown and crisp. You'll need to fry it for 2-3 minutes on each side to get an all-over, even colour. Pour the honey mixture into the pan — it will bubble rapidly — and reduce the heat a little. Working quickly, spoon the liquid over the top of the parcel, until it's all sticky, then remove from the heat. Sprinkle the remaining thyme sprigs and Aleppo pepper over the top and serve.

V

Fried sesame cheese bites

V + GF

Deep-fried cheese? With honey? Obviously, yes. You can use a variety of cheeses here; as long you choose a medium-hard variety, so that the cubes keep their shape when you fry them (but still go a little gooey inside), then you'll be fine. Graviera or kefalotyri are my go-to options, but I also love kefalograviera, halloumi and Mastelo. Sprinkling chilli flakes or slices of green chilli over the top is delightful, but not essential. Honey is essential.

SERVES 4 AS A SNACK

250g graviera or kefalotyri
 (see above)
40g plain flour (use gluten-free,
 if needed)
½ teaspoon sweet smoked paprika
Sea salt and freshly ground
 black pepper
1 large egg
100g sesame seeds
A few sprigs of mint
500ml vegetable oil
3–4 tablespoons honey

Cut the cheese into 1.5–2cm cubes. Place the flour in a shallow dish and mix in the sweet smoked paprika. Season with ½ teaspoon of sea salt and one teaspoon of freshly ground black pepper. Whisk the egg in a second shallow dish with one tablespoon of water until smooth. Place half of the sesame seeds in a third shallow dish. Pick the mint leaves, roughly chop any large ones, and set aside.

Heat the vegetable oil in a wide pan over a medium-high heat to 180°C. Alternatively, place a cube of bread in the oil; when it turns golden-brown, the oil is ready. Toss the cheese cubes in the seasoned flour, then in the beaten egg. Hold the cheese cubes on a fork over the dish to let the excess egg drip off. Place on the sesame-seed plate, sprinkle over the remaining sesame seeds to cover, and gently toss to coat. Transfer the coated cubes of cheese to a clean plate. Line a second plate with kitchen paper.

Fry the cheese for 2–3 minutes, turning halfway through, until deep golden all over. You may need to do this in batches so as not to overcrowd the pan, which will cause the heat to drop and all your cheese to melt away or lose its shape before it's crisp. Lift out the crunchy cheese to the paper-lined plate to absorb any excess oil, then transfer to a serving plate and drizzle with the honey. Sprinkle over a generous pinch of sea salt and a more generous pinch of black pepper. Finish by scattering over the mint leaves and serve straight away.

Whole grilled halloumi with apricots

I'm not very on top of things like social media. I'm hopeless at jumping on bandwagons, always late to the party, trend-wise. However, one thing I did share on social media several years ago now, was my method for scoring and grilling a whole block of halloumi with apricots — it took off. I'd never seen halloumi cooked this way before, and now it's being recreated far and wide and I do feel a bit proud. While the flavour combination is a family standard, I attribute using the whole block to my dear friend Iain, who would eat an entire block of halloumi in one sitting, because 'it looked like a chicken breast'. I thought, well, why can't it be treated like a chicken breast or any other form of protein...? Score, season and grill! Iain, this one's for you.

SERVES 2-4 (OR 1 IAIN)

1 × 250g piece of halloumi
Olive oil
4 apricots
2 tablespoons honey
A few sprigs of oregano or thyme

Preheat your grill to medium-high. Carefully score the top of your halloumi in a criss-cross pattern — don't cut too deep; you want to keep it intact. Rub the cheese with olive oil, in between the cuts, too. Halve the apricots, remove the stones, and halve again into quarters. Place the halloumi in a snug dish (ideally metal) and nestle around the apricots, drizzling them with olive oil, too.

Pop under the grill, not too close, and grill for 8-10 minutes, so that the fruit starts to caramelise and the halloumi is tender and charred on top. The success of this recipe depends on having the right distance from the grill and heat, so check a few minutes into cooking and see if you need to raise the temperature or lower the grill rack. It's quite a forgiving technique, so take your time and see what works with your grill. When the halloumi is ready, drizzle with honey and scatter over the oregano or thyme. Serve immediately.

Figs and dates with anari and rosemary

Make these bombs of deliciousness when you have guests over and want something simple to snack on with a drink. I couldn't decide which I preferred, figs or dates, so I've included both. A ripe, densely flavoured fig is a beautiful thing, but they're not always around and even when they are they're not always great. In that instance, I'll lean towards a plump medjool date. Make whichever works for you.

SERVES 6 AS A SNACK

150g fresh anari or ricotta (strain
 off the liquid if using ricotta)
1 lemon
30g kefalotyri or pecorino
Sea salt and freshly ground
 black pepper
A few sprigs of rosemary
12 figs or medjool dates
2 tablespoons honey
Extra virgin olive oil

Place the anari in a mixing bowl. Finely grate in the lemon zest and the kefalotyri, season generously with sea salt and black pepper and beat till well combined. Taste and adjust the seasoning as needed. Pick and finely chop the rosemary leaves, then set aside. Trim the tips of the figs, then score a cross into the top of each one, cutting through the stalk end, so they still stay connected at the base but open up a little. If using medjool dates, slice into the centre of each and remove the stone, then open them out a little. Spoon a heaped teaspoon of the dressed anari into the middle of the fruits. Drizzle with the honey and some olive oil, then scatter over the chopped rosemary.

A jar of marinated feta, a suggestion

V + GF

This is a loose recipe, a suggestion, because you don't have to do it exactly this way. I've listed my go-to flavours but if I have fresh herbs I might put them in, too. If I'm feeling spice vibes, I'll add a teaspoon each of toasted cumin and coriander seeds. When you next need to pep up salad or a soup, or need a snack on a cracker for a guest, you'll be glad you made this. A jar of marinated feta also makes a fabulous and (almost) effort-free present.

MAKES 1 LARGE JAR

1 × 200g block of feta
2 garlic cloves
½ lemon
½ teaspoon dried oregano or a few
 sprigs of fresh oregano
A few pinches of Aleppo pepper
 (or dried red chilli flakes)
Sea salt and a few black
 peppercorns
Extra virgin olive oil

Have a clean, sterilised jar ready. Cut the feta into 1.5–2cm cubes. Crush the garlic cloves with the side of your knife, keeping them in their skin. Peel strips of lemon rind with a peeler, making sure there isn't any pith on there. Place the feta in the jar, layering it with the crushed garlic cloves, lemon peel, dried or fresh oregano and Aleppo pepper. Add a few pinches of sea salt and peppercorns in there, too. Squeeze in the juice of the lemon half, maybe add a few slices too, and top with enough extra virgin olive oil to cover everything by 1cm. Seal, and store in your fridge for at least a day before using. The feta will keep happily for a few weeks.

Beetroot and dill tzatziki with fried capers

If you have my book *Taverna* you'll know how much I love tzatziki, specifically my mum's recipe, because it is the greatest ever. This is a variation of it. I love the earthy addition of beetroot, the vivid pink-purple colour is so pleasing, and I can never turn down the salty pop of a crisp fried caper. Never, ever. It's a vibrant muddle of excellent ingredients.

SERVES 4-6

½ cucumber or 1 small Middle
  Eastern cucumber
Sea salt and freshly ground
  black pepper
2 cooked beetroot (about 120g)
2 tablespoons olive oil
2 tablespoons capers
250g Greek yoghurt (plant-based,
  if needed)
1 garlic clove
½ bunch of dill
½ lemon

Coarsely grate the cucumber and place in a sieve or colander and toss with ½ teaspoon of the sea salt. Leave over a bowl or in the sink to drain as the salt pulls out the excess moisture. Coarsely grate or chop the beetroot. Stir into the cucumber and leave for 10-15 minutes.

Meanwhile, place a small frying pan or saucepan on a medium-low heat and pour in the olive oil. Fry the capers for about 5 minutes, turning occasionally, until golden and crisp. Leave to one side. Press out the excess liquid from the cucumber-beetroot mix then transfer to a mixing bowl. Stir in the Greek yoghurt and finely grate in the garlic clove, discarding the skin. Finely chop the dill and stir in most of it with the juice of the lemon and half of the fried capers. Taste and adjust the seasoning. Spoon into a serving dish and finish with the remaining dill and fried capers, and a little of the caper cooking oil.

(Photo overleaf)

VG + GF

Sizzling melitzanosalata: *aubergine salad/dip*

When I was a child, I never understood why my yiayia Maroulla had her gas hob lined with foil. It felt a bit 'extra', the same way her Cypriot friends also like to wrap their remote controls in clingfilm or keep a plastic cover on their sofas. What's the point of having nice things if you're going to keep them covered? I now know that lining the hob was different and the woman was a genius, saving herself hours of scrubbing off keftedes grease and aubergine splatters. If you have ever made anything that involves charring vegetables over an open flame, especially aubergine, you'll know the mess is a pain to clean.

This is a classic melitzanosalata recipe (we call it a salad; you might think it's more of a dip), but with a hot dressing. I love the method of pouring hot oil over raw garlic and spices; it takes off the very pungent, raw edge, but still keeps things fragrant and punchy. I'll always choose the option for more garlic, but if you prefer it milder, use one clove.

SERVES 6

3 aubergines
Sea salt and freshly ground
 black pepper
1 tablespoon sesame seeds
3 tablespoons tahini
1 lemon
1–2 garlic cloves, depending how
 punchy you like it
½ teaspoon Aleppo pepper (or
 ¼ teaspoon dried red chilli flakes)
½ teaspoon dried oregano, plus
 extra to serve
5 tablespoons olive oil

VG + GF

You can char the aubergines on the hob or under the grill. Cook the aubergines directly over a flame, for about 10–15 minutes, turning until they are blackened all over. If you do them under a grill, they should take the same amount of time, but keep an eye on the temperature of the grill and height of the tray. When they are blackened on the outside and tender within, place the aubergines in a mixing bowl, cover and leave for 5 minutes to steam. This will help the charred skin come off easily. Peel when still warm, then roughly chop the flesh. Mix it with one teaspoon of sea salt and place in a colander in the sink or over the mixing bowl to get rid of any excess liquid. In a small pan on a medium heat, toast the sesame seeds until golden. Set aside and leave to cool.

After 30 minutes, transfer the aubergine flesh back to the cleaned mixing bowl and mash until it is creamy, but still has a little texture. (You can do this in a food processor, but I don't like mine too smooth, so I don't.) Beat in the tahini and juice of the lemon. Season to taste — it will be salty, but check if it needs a little more. Spoon the purée onto a serving plate and finely grate over the garlic. Sprinkle with the Aleppo pepper and oregano. Just before serving, heat the olive oil in a small pan over a medium heat until it is sizzling, then pour over the top of the aubergines so that the garlic sizzles. Leave the oil to cool for 1 minute, then stir into the aubergines. You can serve this straight away, topped with the toasted sesame seeds and a little more oregano, or leave the flavours to develop.

(Photo overleaf)

Clockwise from top left: herby skordalia (page 79); everything pita chips (page 80); beetroot and dill tzatziki with fried capers (page 74); sizzling melitzanosalata (page 75); artichoke houmous (page 78)

Artichoke houmous

This is my classic houmous, but with the addition of grilled or marinated deli artichokes — a simple but fabulous twist. I've said it before, but there's a huge difference between jarred and tinned chickpeas, and you really notice it when you make houmous. A jarred chickpea will give you a creamier finish, so if you can, choose them. They range from wildly expensive in fancy delis, to cheaper than chips in international supermarkets, but they're essentially all the same, so get whatever you can afford.

SERVES 6

1 × 400g jar or tin of chickpeas
200g grilled or marinated
 artichokes in olive oil
3 tablespoons tahini
½ lemon
1 garlic clove
Sea salt and freshly ground
 black pepper

Drain the chickpeas, but reserve the liquid, and place them in a food processor with the artichokes (again, reserving the olive oil). Add the tahini and juice of the lemon half. Peel and roughly chop the garlic and add to the food processor with three tablespoons of the chickpea liquid. Blitz until incredibly smooth, adding more of the chickpea liquid as needed until you have a smooth, mousse-like texture. Season to taste — you will need to be generous. Transfer to a serving plate or bowl and finish with a good drizzle of the artichoke oil.

(Photo on page 76)

VG + GF

Herby skordalia: *garlic dip*

Skordo is the Greek word for garlic, so do not be shocked at how garlicky this dip is. I'm talking spicy, punch-in-the-face levels of garlic. It's sometimes made on a base of stale bread or nuts, but I prefer it with potato; the herbs are not traditional, but I like the added flavour and freshness they bring. This is easy to make, a great foil to grilled meat, fish and veg — and incredibly addictive. You'll keep going back for another swipe.

SERVES 6

2 baking potatoes (about 500g)
5 garlic cloves — I use raw garlic, but if you're nervous you can use roasted cloves, for a milder, sweeter finish
1 teaspoon sea salt
1 bunch of soft herbs (mint, chives, flat-leaf parsley)
½ bunch of spring onions
1 lemon
150ml vegetable or light olive oil

Peel your potatoes and cut them into equal-sized pieces. Bring a large pan of salted water to the boil and add the potato chunks. Reduce the heat a little and simmer for 12–15 minutes, depending on how big the chunks are. They need to be cooked through and soft. Drain in a colander, reserve a mug of the water, and leave the potatoes to steam-dry for a few minutes.

While the potatoes are cooking, peel the garlic. You want to crush it to a paste; I like to use a pestle and mortar to smash it with the sea salt until creamy. Alternatively, finely grate into a small bowl with the sea salt. Pick and finely chop the herbs. Trim and finely chop the spring onions.

When the potatoes have cooled just a little, mash them until smooth — if you have a potato ricer, or even a sieve, pressing them through this is ideal. If you need to, use a little of the hot cooking water to make it as smooth as possible. Beat in the garlic, the juice of half the lemon and then slowly beat in the vegetable or light olive oil. When all the oil is in, mix hard and fast until you have a smooth, thick sauce. Finish by stirring in the chopped herbs and spring onions. Taste to check the seasoning, adding more salt or lemon juice as needed, then serve.

(Photo on page 76)

VG + GF

Everything pita chips

When you have a few stale pita breads kicking about, or just want to make a batch of snacks, this is the recipe you should turn to. The 'everything' label here is my Greek twist on the seasonings in New York's everything bagels. These chips are delicious with dips on their own, and they'd even make great croutons in a salad. As long as you cool them completely before you store them in an airtight container, they'll last for ages.

SERVES 4–6

2 teaspoons dried oregano
2 teaspoons sesame seeds
1 teaspoon black sesame seeds
½ teaspoon Aleppo pepper (or
 ¼ teaspoon dried red chilli flakes)
1 teaspoon garlic powder
Sea salt and freshly ground
 black pepper
4 large pita (gluten-free,
 if needed)
Olive oil

Preheat your oven to 210°C/190°C fan/gas mark 6½. Mix together the dried oregano, sesame seeds, Aleppo pepper and garlic powder. Season well; use about ½ teaspoon each of salt and pepper. Cut the pita into 3–4cm lengths, about 2cm wide, and open each piece out from the cut centre. Place all the pita in a bowl and drizzle well with olive oil. Sprinkle with the spice blend and toss everything together to really get the flavours to stick. Spread the pita out in one layer on a baking sheet (you may need to use two sheets) and pop the tray(s) in the oven. Bake for 10–12 minutes, until they are golden all over. Leave the chips to cool completely on the tray and store in an airtight container until needed.

(Photo on page 76)

VG + GF

Vegetables

Charred cabbage, lemon and rice soup

Understated lentils with halloumi

Skordostoumbi pasta: roasted aubergine, tomato, garlic
 and feta pasta

Sticky aubergine, pomegranate and herb tart

Mushroom and lentil hilopites

SAS: Spanakopita Appreciation Society

Spanakopita jacket potatoes

Spanakorisotto

Spanakopita fritters

Seafood

Sticky honey prawns

Mussels in saffron yoghurt

Sole bourdeto with new potatoes

Barbecued sea bass stuffed with pistachio and caper pesto

Tuna, egg and caper salad

Meat

Lemon and oregano chicken with a feta dip, two ways

- Addictive wings
- One-pot chicken thighs and rice

Village pasta with chicken and lemon

Halloumi fried chicken

HLT kritharaki

Braised sausage, lentils and fennel

One-pan pastitsio

Classic biftekia and chips

Little lamb meatballs with chickpeas

Spiced lamb chops with houmous

Everyday heroes

Charred cabbage, lemon and rice soup

When I was growing up, my mum would often make us krambosoupa, which translates as 'cabbage soup'. I've never been able to find another Greek or Cypriot recipe similar to hers, which makes it all the more special. Her version is simple and clean, with piercing lines of flavour from copious lemon juice and good extra virgin olive oil. I've tweaked it slightly here, by charring the cabbage first to give it a little added savoury depth, and adding dill for freshness (or flat-leaf parsley, if you prefer). However, when I am feeling particularly nostalgic and in need of comfort I'll revert back to my mum's classic method. Or I just ask her to make it for me.

SERVES 6-8

800g white cabbage
  (a medium cabbage)
4 onions
2 garlic cloves
Olive oil
Sea salt and freshly ground
  black pepper
130g long grain rice
1 teaspoon caster sugar
2 litres vegetable stock
2 lemons
½ bunch of dill (optional)

Place a griddle pan on a high heat, and get it hot. Cut the cabbage into wedges about 3cm thick. Place on the hot griddle pan, and cook for 3-4 minutes on each side until charred. Do this in batches if needed.

Meanwhile, peel and finely chop the onions and garlic. Place a large saucepan on a medium heat and add four tablespoons of olive oil. Add the onions, season and sauté for 10 minutes, to really get them glossy and softened and starting to brown at the edges. Stir in the chopped garlic, cook for a couple of minutes, then stir in the rice and caster sugar. After a minute, pour in the vegetable stock and bring to the boil.

By now the cabbage should be ready. Transfer the cabbage wedges to the chopping board and, once cool enough to handle, roughly chop. Add the cabbage to the pot. Once everything is boiling, cover with the lid, reduce to low and cook for 20 minutes — the rice and cabbage should be tender. Squeeze in the juice from the lemons and tweak the seasoning to your taste. Leave to cool for 5 minutes. Finely chop the dill, if using, and stir through before serving.

Understated lentils with halloumi

V + GF

This dish is a love child of two famous Greek and Cypriot dishes — faki (fakes) and trahana. Faki is a lentil and rice dish that varies throughout both countries, but is always quite oozy and stew-like. Trahana is a soup made from yoghurt and wheat that has been fermented and dried. It is both sour and creamy, and in Cyprus we eat it with vermicelli and halloumi. It can be hard to track down, and is an acquired taste. Both dishes are simple fare, but comforting. I've pulled the best elements from each to create a recipe that's simple, soothing, balanced — quietly complete.

SERVES 4

4 onions
50g unsalted butter
Olive oil
Sea salt and freshly ground
  black pepper
175g green lentils
75g vermicelli (or use fine
  gluten-free pasta or rice noodles)
1 tablespoon tomato purée
1 ½ teaspoons dried mint
150g halloumi
1 tablespoon honey

Peel and finely slice the onions. Place a large saucepan or casserole on a medium heat and add the butter and a drizzle of olive oil. Add the onions, season well and sauté for at least 10 minutes, until it all starts to soften. If you can give it longer, you will be rewarded with an intensely sweet, richer soup. If you only have 10 minutes, it will still be good.

While the onions are cooking, wash and turn the lentils in a sieve under cold running water and pick out any stones. Break the vermicelli into small pieces. When the onions are ready, stir in the vermicelli and turn the heat up a little. You want the pasta to get a little colour. After a few minutes, add the tomato purée and one teaspoon of the dried mint, stir in for a minute or two, then add the washed lentils. Pour over 1.25 litres of cold water and bring to the boil. Cover, reduce the heat to low and simmer for 35-40 minutes, until everything is soft. Cut the halloumi into 1-1.5cm cubes and stir two-thirds of them into the soup. Season generously and continue to cook for a further 5 minutes, until creamy.

Just before the soup is ready, place a small frying pan on a medium heat and drizzle in a few tablespoons of olive oil. Fry the remaining halloumi cubes for a couple of minutes until they are golden and a little crisp on all sides. Stir the remaining ½ teaspoon of dried mint into the soup, then ladle it out into bowls. Drizzle the halloumi with honey and divide it between the bowls of soup. Eat immediately.

Skordostoumbi pasta: *roasted aubergine, tomato, garlic and feta pasta*

V + GF

Skordostoumbi is a dish found in the Ionian islands. It's layers of aubergine and tomato, and heavy on the garlic — the name means garlic cloves. It is traditionally a vegan dish, but here I've roasted it in the oven, surrounding a block of feta. It's super simple but looks impressive, and makes an excellent sauce for pasta. If you want to keep it plant-based, just leave out the feta — it's still delicious.

SERVES 4

1 aubergine
6 garlic cloves
400g cherry tomatoes
1 teaspoon caster sugar
1 teaspoon Aleppo pepper (or
 ½ teaspoon dried red chilli flakes)
1 teaspoon dried oregano
Sea salt and freshly ground
 black pepper
5 tablespoons olive oil
2 tablespoons red wine vinegar
1 × 200g block of feta
350g spaghetti or linguine
 (gluten-free, if needed)
½ bunch of basil

Preheat your oven to 200°C/180°C fan/gas mark 6. Trim the aubergine and peel off most of the skin — I use a peeler to remove it in strips. Cut the flesh into 2cm cubes and place in a large roasting tray. Crush the garlic cloves with the side of your knife, leaving them in their skins. Add to the tray with the cherry tomatoes, caster sugar, Aleppo pepper and most of the dried oregano. Season everything generously and drizzle with four tablespoons of the olive oil and all the red wine vinegar. Really massage in the flavours. Nestle the feta in the middle of all the ingredients, drizzle with the remaining olive oil, scatter over the rest of the dried oregano and pop the tray into the oven. Roast for 40–45 minutes, until the vegetables are charred and blistered and the feta is golden around the edges.

When the vegetables are almost ready, bring a large saucepan of salted water to the boil. Cook the pasta according to the packet instructions until al dente (or how you like it). Pick and roughly tear or chop the basil leaves. When the pasta is nearly done, remove the tray from the oven. Scoop out about 200ml of the starchy pasta water and mix with the vegetables and feta in the tray, really crushing in the garlic (removing the skins) and breaking up the feta. Drain the pasta, reserving the water. Toss the pasta through the tray, adding a further 100–150ml of the pasta water, until the juices are creamy and oozy. Finish with the torn basil leaves and serve straight away.

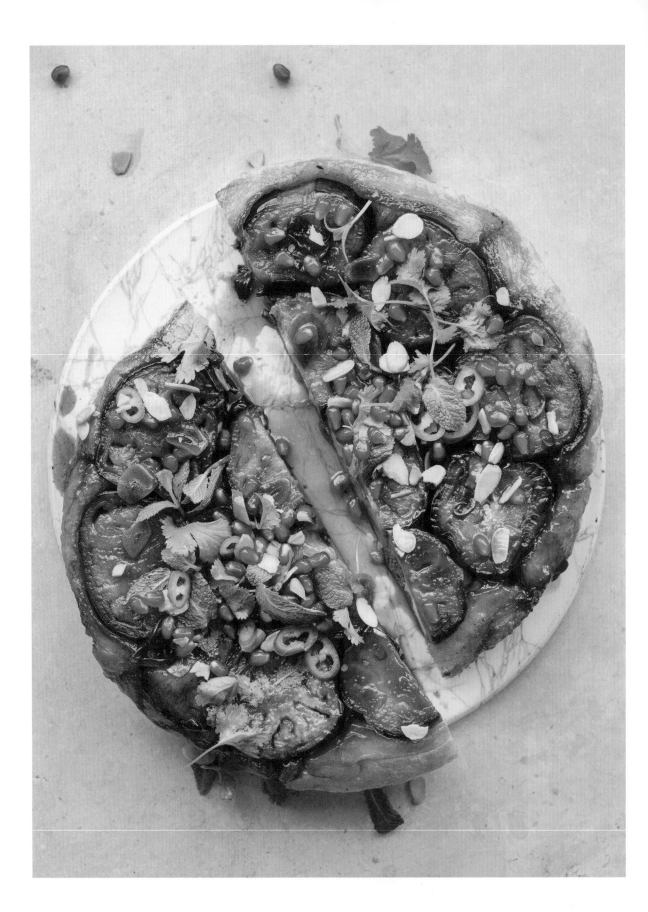

Sticky aubergine, pomegranate and herb tart

There was a time in this country when aubergines weren't getting the full love and cooking attention they need. It was a time of tough, rubbery, undercooked aubs (often seen with stuffed peppers and abundant, very average mushroom risotto). This was confusing for teenage vegetarian me, as I'd always eaten delicious, tender aubergines at home. My yiayias knew they needed fat (and lots of it) and a long cooking time. Although I haven't been served a rubbery aubergine for a while, for many people they're still an intimidating vegetable to cook at home. Fear not. This upside-down tart is a simple way to nail the dense but yielding texture that makes good aubergine dishes so desirable. It is vegan, if you use dairy-free pastry, and lacking in no way (but you could crumble over some feta if you like) and makes a fantastic centrepiece to impress guests.

SERVES 4

2 large or 3 medium aubergines
20g flaked almonds
4 tablespoons olive oil
2 garlic cloves
1–2 green chillies
3 tablespoons pomegranate
  molasses
2 tablespoons red wine vinegar
2 tablespoons caster sugar
500g puff pastry (plant-based,
  if needed)
½ pomegranate
½ bunch each of coriander
  and mint

Preheat your oven to 220°C/200°C fan/gas mark 7. Trim the aubergines, use a peeler to remove some of the skin in strips and slice the flesh into 2.5cm rounds. Place a large ovenproof frying pan or shallow casserole (about 30cm in diameter) on a medium heat and toast the flaked almonds for a few minutes, until golden. Remove from the pan and set aside. Add three tablespoons of the olive oil to the pan and, in batches if needed, fry the aubergine slices for about 3 minutes on each side until lightly browned. Add more oil as you go, if needed.

Peel and finely slice the garlic and finely slice the chillies. Whisk the pomegranate molasses, red wine vinegar, caster sugar, garlic and half the chilli together in a small bowl. When the aubergine is ready, remove to a plate. Pour the pomegranate sauce into the pan, bring to the boil, then simmer for 2 minutes, until reduced and sticky. Remove from the heat and replace the aubergine slices in the pan. Roll out the puff pastry so it is a bit larger than the pan, drape it over the top and carefully tuck down the inside of the pan. Prick the top with a fork and place the pan in the oven for 25 minutes, until deep golden on top and bubbling at the edges.

While the tart is in the oven, pick the pomegranate seeds and pick and roughly chop the herbs. Toss with the remaining sliced green chilli and toasted flaked almonds. When the tart is ready, remove and leave to rest for a minute before carefully turning out on a board or platter. Sprinkle over the herby pomegranate and nuts, then slice and serve.

VG

Mushroom and lentil hilopites

This dish started life as my attempt at making a vegan ragu to rival my much-loved (by my family) Greek bolognese (see the pastitsio recipe on page 124 for an idea of how to make it). When I tell you this recipe had people fooled, I'm not exaggerating. The texture of blitzed-up mushrooms really does feel like mince. Here I cook the ragu with hilopites, little squares of pasta that are popular in Greece. You can leave it out, then toss the ragu through whatever pasta you like. To make it vegan, you can easily leave out the cream and cheese at the end, or use a plant-based variety.

SERVES 4

2 onions

2 carrots

2 garlic cloves

2 celery sticks

4 sprigs of rosemary

5 tablespoons olive oil

300g chestnut mushrooms

Sea salt and freshly ground
  black pepper

2 tablespoons tomato purée

1 teaspoon ground cinnamon

1 teaspoon caster sugar

1 × 400g tin of green lentils,
  including liquid

200g hilopites, or broken-up
  tagliatelle (gluten-free, if needed)

1 litre vegetable stock

Extra virgin olive oil

A splash of double cream
  (plant-based cream works well)

Grated hard cheese, to finish
  (optional)

Peel the onions, carrots and garlic. Trim the celery and pull the rosemary leaves off the stalks. Place everything in the bowl of a food processor and blitz until finely chopped. You can, of course, do this by hand, but it's a lot quicker if you have a food processor. Scrape into a wide saucepan or casserole with the olive oil and sauté on a medium-low heat for 10 minutes.

Meanwhile, wipe the mushrooms and place in the same food processor bowl (no need to clean it) and blitz until you have a fine, mince-like texture. Again, you can do this by hand, but it'll take a long time and might be less convincingly like mince. Add the mushrooms to the pan, turn up the heat a little, and season well. Fry for a further 10 minutes, then add the tomato purée, cinnamon and sugar. Stir in and fry for a minute, then add the lentils (the liquid too), hilopites and vegetable stock. Bring to the boil, drizzle in a few tablespoons of extra virgin olive oil and cover with a lid. Reduce to a simmer and cook for about 30 minutes, stirring only a couple of times.

When it is ready — when the pasta is very tender and the sauce is thickened — remove from the heat and leave to rest for 5 minutes. Serve either as is or with a little ripple of cream, a drizzle of extra virgin olive oil and grated cheese over the top.

SAS: Spanakopita Appreciation Society

Spanakopita, the famous spinach and cheese pie, is a beautiful thing, and since learning my yiayia's method of salting (not wilting) the spinach filling, I love it even more. I wrote about this process, plus the pie, in my book *Taverna*, but you can also read about it on page 100 in my spanakopita fritters. Essentially, instead of wilting the spinach over heat, you withdraw the moisture from the leaves by salting and then squeezing it out. It keeps the leaves vibrant and so much more flavoursome.

Since then, I have fallen down a spinach-feta rabbit hole, constantly wondering what else could I make? What else can I spanakopita-fy? The possibilities are endless. There have been risottos, fritters, stuffed jacket potatoes; I even played with scones, pasta and salads. (Perhaps I have just given away my theme for book five.) Most of my experiments were a success, especially with my daughters — spinach and cheese is an almost universally popular combination.

The recipes that follow are yours for the shaping. Add a little Aleppo pepper if you enjoy heat. Or extra lemon zest and juice if you like things a bit tart. If you love your jacket potatoes obscenely cheesy, like me, feel free to add as much as you can bear. The risotto is elegant, classy even, but also easy enough for a regular Tuesday night. The fritters make a perfect light lunch, or fry them up small as part of a meze spread. These recipes are all versatile, and much quicker and easier than making a full pie. Meaning you can get your spanakopita hit more often.

Spanakopita jacket potatoes

V + GF

Like many parents, I am always trying to get my kids to eat more vegetables, so making dishes 'spanakopita-ish' has become a go-to method for us (if in doubt, add cheese). In this instance, it is the reliable jacket potato that gets the cheese and spinach treatment. This isn't a short recipe, but it is straightforward. The majority of the cooking is baking the spuds, which can be done in advance. You can even make the filled jacket potatoes the day before, or when cooking another dish, and leave them stuffed and covered in the fridge until you need dinner, in which case simply bake until bubbling and delicious.

SERVES 4

4 baking potatoes
Olive oil
100g baby spinach
¼ bunch of flat-leaf parsley or dill, or a combination
1 bunch of spring onions
150g graviera or mature cheddar
Sea salt and freshly ground black pepper
40g unsalted butter
3 tablespoons Greek yoghurt
½ lemon
1 green chilli
100g feta

Preheat your oven to 200°C/180°C fan/gas mark 6. Prick the potatoes all over with a fork and rub with a little olive oil. Wrap in foil and bake for about 1 hour, until the potatoes are tender all the way through. Remove from the oven and leave for 15 minutes, until just cool enough to handle.

Meanwhile, finely chop the spinach, flat-leaf parsley and/or dill, then trim and finely slice the spring onions. Coarsely grate the graviera or cheddar. Halve each potato and scoop the middles into a large mixing bowl and season generously with sea salt and black pepper. Mash in the butter then add the sliced spinach, spring onions and most of the parsley/dill. Stir in the yoghurt and two-thirds of the grated cheese, and finely grate in the lemon zest. Divide the mixture back between the potato shells.

Finely slice the green chilli, removing the seeds if you don't want too much spice, and place in a bowl. Crumble in the feta and toss together with the remaining grated cheese and a little drizzle of olive oil. Scatter this over the potatoes and place back in the oven for 25 minutes, until the cheese is golden and bubbling. I sometimes like to finish it under a hot grill for 5-10 minutes to get the top super golden and toasted. Scatter with the remaining herbs and serve.

Spanakorisotto

V + GF

Spanakorizo is a popular Greek rice dish, laced with spinach and tomatoes. It isn't oozy like a risotto, as it's usually made with a slightly longer grain rice. But just because it isn't traditionally like that doesn't mean it can't be. Creamy instead of tomato-based. All the cheese. All the spinach. I present to you: spanakorisotto.

SERVES 4–6

1.5 litres vegetable stock
2 leeks
1 onion
60g unsalted butter
Olive oil
A few sprigs of oregano
Sea salt and freshly ground
 black pepper
400g risotto rice
150ml white wine
75g kefalotyri, parmesan or
 vegetarian hard cheese
½ lemon
½ bunch of flat-leaf parsley
150g baby spinach
100g feta

Bring the stock to a simmer in a saucepan and leave on a low heat. Trim and finely slice the leeks, then give them a good wash in a colander to get rid of any mud. Halve, peel and finely chop the onion. Place a wide pan or pot on a medium-low heat and add half the butter, a drizzle of olive oil, the sliced leeks and chopped onion. Pick in the oregano leaves, season well and sauté for 10 minutes.

Stir in the rice and cook for a minute or two, making sure it gets glossy and coated in the oil, and then add the wine. Turn up the heat, bring to the boil and keep stirring until the rice has absorbed all the wine. Reduce the heat back to medium-low and add a ladleful of hot stock and stir it in. Only ladle in more stock once the previous lot has been absorbed. While the rice is cooking, in between stirs, finely grate the kefalotyri and lemon zest and finely chop the flat-leaf parsley. Keep ladling and stirring and ladling. Chop the baby spinach. The rice should take about 20-25 minutes. When it is almost ready (check by eating a grain; it will be tender but still have a bit of a bite to it), stir in the chopped spinach and keep cooking.

When the rice is tender all the way through, stir in the lemon zest, chopped parsley and most of the kefalotyri. Pop in the remaining butter and cover with a lid to rest for a few minutes. When ready, stir in a squeeze of lemon juice and ladle onto serving plates. Finish by crumbling over the feta and scattering with the last of the kefalotyri.

Spanakopita fritters

V + GF

I love the ease of these fritters; they're great as a light meal with a little salad, for a starter or even shaped a little smaller and cooked as a snack or party bite. For extra body, I've added courgette to the spinach. You can wilt the spinach in a hot pan, but I am a die-hard 'salt the spinach leaves to wilt them' woman. It takes a bit longer but I think it gives the best texture and flavour. (You could also use frozen spinach for this recipe.)

SERVES 4

100g baby spinach
1 large courgette
1 teaspoon sea salt
½ bunch of dill, mint or flat-leaf
 parsley — or a combination
4 spring onions
100g plain flour (gluten-free,
 if needed)
1 teaspoon baking powder
Freshly ground black pepper
2 large eggs
50g Greek yoghurt
100g feta
Olive oil
1 lemon, to serve

Roughly chop the spinach and place in a colander set in the sink. Trim and coarsely grate in the courgette, add to the colander and toss the vegetables with the sea salt. Mix together well and leave for 15-20 minutes to draw out the moisture. Give the mixture a good squeeze to really extract all the water, then transfer to a large mixing bowl. Finely chop the herbs, trim and finely slice the spring onions, and add both to the bowl. Stir in the plain flour, baking powder and a good pinch of black pepper. Beat in the eggs and yoghurt. Crumble and fold in the feta.

Line a plate with kitchen paper. Place a large frying pan on a medium heat. Pour in enough olive oil to just cover the base. Spoon in the fritters, one heaped tablespoon of the batter at a time — don't crowd the pan. Fry for 3-4 minutes on each side until golden and crisp, then transfer to the paper-lined plate. Keep frying until all the mixture is fried. Serve with a generous pinch of salt on top, and lemon wedges for squeezing over.

Sticky honey prawns

DF + GF

I discovered a variation of this recipe during my research for *Nistisima* (my previous book) in a book called *Culinaria Greece* by Marianthi Milona. I'd never heard of prawns being cooked with honey and was intrigued. In addition, fish sauce was something I had never seen used in Greek food before. After much research I realised it probably referenced 'garum', a fermented fish sauce that was used in Ancient Greece and Rome. There are people today who make their own versions, and it seems like it isn't too dissimilar to the commonly found fish sauce used in south-east Asian cooking (or even Worcestershire sauce). This truly delicious, genuinely speedy recipe has become a new staple in our house.

SERVES 4

2 onions
1 green chilli
500g peeled, raw king prawns
½ bunch of oregano or thyme
3 tablespoons olive oil
2 tablespoons fish sauce
2 tablespoons honey
½ teaspoon freshly ground
 black pepper
½ lemon, plus wedges to serve
 (optional)

Peel and finely slice the onions. Halve, deseed and finely slice the chilli. Devein and butterfly the prawns, if they aren't already done. Pick the oregano or thyme leaves. Place a large frying pan on a medium heat and add the olive oil. Add the onions and sauté for 10 minutes. Add the chilli, the prawns and herbs. Fry for a couple of minutes, then add the fish sauce, honey and black pepper. Squeeze in the lemon juice and turn up the heat. Leave to bubble away for 4-5 minutes, until the prawns are cooked and the sauce is thickened and sticky. Serve immediately, with lemon wedges for squeezing, if you like.

Mussels in saffron yoghurt

Mussels are such a great choice for a quick weeknight meal, and always feel a bit fancy to me. (And grown-up — oh, I can eat shellfish any time I like?) A pile of steaming mussels, a crusty fresh baguette and a glass of wine — so chic. Throw in a warm sunny evening and it's hard to be happier. I tested this recipe in several ways, and wanted to keep it as simple as possible. Spooning out the mussels and reducing the sauce is an extra step, but to get the maximum intensity of flavour, it's worth the very minor bother.

SERVES 2

1kg mussels
A good pinch of saffron
2 shallots
2 garlic cloves
½ bunch of flat-leaf parsley
50g unsalted butter
Olive oil
150ml white wine
300ml chicken or seafood stock
200g Greek yoghurt
Sea salt and freshly ground
 black pepper
A few sprigs of dill (optional)

Give the mussels a good clean: rinse in fresh water, remove any beards or stringy bits and throw away any that are broken or are open and don't close when you tap them.

Place the saffron in a small bowl and top with a splash of boiling water and leave to one side. Peel and finely chop the shallots and garlic. Finely chop the parsley stalks and then the leaves, keeping them separate. Place a large saucepan on a medium-low heat and add the butter, a drizzle of oil, the shallots, garlic and parsley stalks and sauté for 5 minutes. Add the wine, increase the heat and bring to the boil. Reduce the wine so that it is almost all cooked away, then add the stock. Bring to the boil, stir in the mussels and cover with a lid. Reduce the heat a little and cook for about 6 minutes, until the mussels are cooked. When the mussels have all opened, remove the pan from the heat, and lift out the mussels with a slotted spoon or spider to a large serving bowl.

Return the saucepan with the cooking liquor to the heat and boil until reduced by a third. Remove from the heat. Stir the saffron water into the yoghurt, then stir the yoghurt into the broth. Taste for seasoning; it might not need any extra. Pour the broth over the mussels in the serving bowl. Finely chop the dill, if using, and scatter over the mussels with the chopped parsley leaves, then serve.

Sole bourdeto with new potatoes

DF + GF

This is a simple recipe with great impact, thanks in part to a good hit of spice. It originates in Corfu and appears to have been inspired by Venetian brodetto (meaning broth). You can use any fish on top: whatever is sustainable, that you can find and, most importantly, like. Something mild, to take on the punchy juices, would be perfect.

SERVES 2

2 red onions
2 garlic cloves
3 tablespoons olive oil
1 teaspoon fennel seeds
1 tablespoon sweet smoked
 paprika
1 teaspoon Aleppo pepper (or ½
 teaspoon dried red chilli flakes)
Sea salt and freshly ground
 black pepper
400g new potatoes
1 tablespoon tomato purée
1 lemon
250g lemon sole fillets
½ bunch of flat-leaf parsley

Peel and finely chop the red onions and garlic. Place a deep frying pan or shallow saucepan, one large enough to hold the fish fillets, on a medium heat and add the olive oil. Add the chopped onions and garlic and cook for 5 minutes. Finely crush the fennel seeds, then stir into the onions along with the paprika and Aleppo pepper, and season well. Reduce the heat a little and cook for a further 10 minutes.

Meanwhile, slice the new potatoes into 1.5cm rounds. When the onions are ready, stir in the tomato purée and fry for a minute, then add the sliced potatoes. Squeeze over the juice of the lemon and pour over enough water to cover almost everything. Bring to the boil, then reduce the heat just a little so that the liquid is gently bubbling away. Cover and cook for 10 minutes.

Lay the lemon sole on top of the potatoes; cover again and cook for a further 5 minutes. Remove the lid, turn up the heat and cook on high for 3 minutes, until everything is tender and most of the liquid has cooked away. Finely chop the parsley, scatter over the top and serve.

Barbecued sea bass stuffed with pistachio and caper pesto

DF + GF

I started making this recipe for my pescatarian family when they'd come over for a barbecue. They love a prawn kebab, but it's nice to mix things up and sea bass is glorious cooked over hot coals. Serving a whole fish feels decadent, like you've gone to great effort, but it's very straightforward — the end result tastes more complex than the method. The pistachio and caper pesto can be used in myriad dishes, cooked or not.

SERVES 2

½ bunch of mint
1 garlic clove
½ teaspoon fennel seeds
A large handful of pistachios
2 tablespoons capers
½ teaspoon Aleppo pepper (or
  ¼ teaspoon dried red chilli flakes)
1 lemon
Sea salt and freshly ground
  black pepper
3 tablespoons olive oil, plus
  a little extra
2 whole sea bass, gutted, cleaned
  and scaled (or 4 sea bass fillets,
  which you can stuff then tie
  together with string)

Start by making the stuffing. Pick the mint leaves. Peel and chop the garlic. Roughly crush the fennel seeds. Place the pistachios in a food processor with the chopped garlic, crushed fennel seeds, capers, Aleppo pepper and most of the mint leaves. Finely grate in the lemon zest. Season generously. Pulse everything together until roughly chopped. Add two tablespoons of olive oil and pulse again until you have a rough paste — chopped enough to hold together and not too fine. Taste a little and adjust the seasoning.

Place your sea bass on a chopping board and slash the skin on each side two or three times. Rub all over with a little olive oil and season the cavity and skin. Keep the stuffing in the food processor bowl, and spoon a few tablespoons into the middle of each fish, really stuffing it in. Tie the fish up with string, to stop the filling falling out. Squeeze the juice from half the lemon into the food processor bowl, add another tablespoon of olive oil and blitz the remaining pistachio mix into a smooth paste. (You can do all this ahead of cooking; just cover and store the fish in the fridge until needed.)

Get your barbecue ready. Cook the fish over hot coals for 8-10 minutes on each side, until charred and cooked through; keep an eye on them. Alternatively, preheat your oven to 210°C/190°C fan/gas mark 6½, and roast your fish for 20-25 minutes. Spoon the smooth pistachio paste onto a serving platter and place the charred sea bass on top. Cut the remaining lemon half into wedges, serve next to the fish and finish by scattering over the remaining mint leaves.

Tuna, egg and caper salad

DF + GF

I ate a very similar salad to this in Thessaloniki, a Greek salad niçoise if you will, and nothing has ever tasted more like a Mediterranean summer. I make mine with fresh tuna when I can, but it works as well with good-quality tinned or jarred tuna in olive oil.

SERVES 2

300g waxy potatoes, Cyprus
 variety ideally
2 large eggs
½ red onion
3 tablespoons red wine vinegar
Sea salt and freshly ground
 black pepper
2 tablespoons capers
1 teaspoon honey
3 tablespoons extra virgin olive oil
1 avocado
250g tuna steak
Olive oil
A couple of pinches of dried
 oregano
40g wild rocket

Wash the potatoes and place, unpeeled, in a saucepan. Cover with water and bring to the boil, then reduce the heat a little and simmer for 12–15 minutes or until the potatoes are tender. As soon as they are done, drain and leave them in the hot pan to cool slightly. I add the eggs to the pan at the same time as the potatoes, then lift them out after 7 minutes and plunge them into cold water.

Meanwhile, peel and finely slice the red onion. Place in a large mixing bowl and toss with the red wine vinegar and a generous pinch of sea salt. Stir the capers and honey into the onion, followed by the extra virgin olive oil. When the potatoes are cool enough to handle but still quite warm, cut into 1.5cm slices and toss through the onion and caper dressing. Halve the avocado, remove the stone and cut into 1cm slices. Gently stir into the potatoes.

Place a large frying pan on a high heat. Rub the tuna steak with a little olive oil and the dried oregano, and season well. Pop the steak in the pan and sear for 3 minutes on each side, so it has a lovely deep crust but is still slightly pink in the middle. Transfer to a chopping board and leave to rest for a couple of minutes. Meanwhile, toss the rocket with the potatoes and avocado. Peel the eggs and cut into wedges. Slice or flake the tuna into pieces and stir both into the salad. Serve straight away.

Lemon and oregano chicken with a feta dip, two ways

I honestly don't think there is a chicken marinade I love more than lemon and oregano, with proper seasoning and plenty of olive oil. But which way to go... Crispy wings? Or letting the juices drizzle into rice as more of a meal? In the end, I decided I didn't actually need to decide — you're getting both. One is more a snack, one is definitely a meal, and both will satisfy your need for crisp, tangy, lip-smacking chook.

GF

Addictive wings

SERVES 4, OR 8 AS A SNACK

1kg chicken wings
2 lemons
2 tablespoons olive oil, plus a little
  extra for frying
2 teaspoons garlic powder
2 teaspoons dried oregano
2 teaspoons sea salt
1 teaspoon freshly ground
  black pepper
2 red chillies
1 garlic clove
200g feta
150g Greek yoghurt
100g mayonnaise
40g kefalotyri or pecorino

Preheat your oven to 220°C/200°C fan/gas mark 7. You want your chicken wings to be jointed into drumettes and flats. If yours didn't come prepared this way, chop each wing down the main joint to separate (see page 271).

Place the chicken wings in a large mixing bowl. Finely grate in the zest from one lemon. Squeeze in the juice, then add the olive oil, garlic powder, oregano, sea salt and black pepper. Toss together well, really massaging the flavours into the chicken. Line a baking sheet with greaseproof paper and spread the wings out in one layer. Roast for 35–45 minutes, turning halfway through, until well cooked and deep golden-brown.

While the wings are roasting, make the dip. Halve, deseed and finely slice the chillies. Peel and finely slice the garlic. Place a small pan on a medium heat, add enough oil to just cover the base and fry the chilli and garlic for a minute or so, just till lightly golden, then remove from the heat. Break the feta up in a bowl and mash in the Greek yoghurt. Using a fork will be easiest; it'll be a little grainy but keep going. Stir in the mayonnaise and finely grate in the kefalotyri. Finely grate in the zest of the remaining lemon. Stir the fried chilli and garlic into the feta dip and squeeze in the juice of half of the remaining lemon. Mix everything well. Taste and adjust the seasoning, adding more lemon, salt and pepper if needed.

When the wings are ready, transfer to a platter with a bowl of the dipping sauce. I like to serve this with some chunky sticks of cucumber.

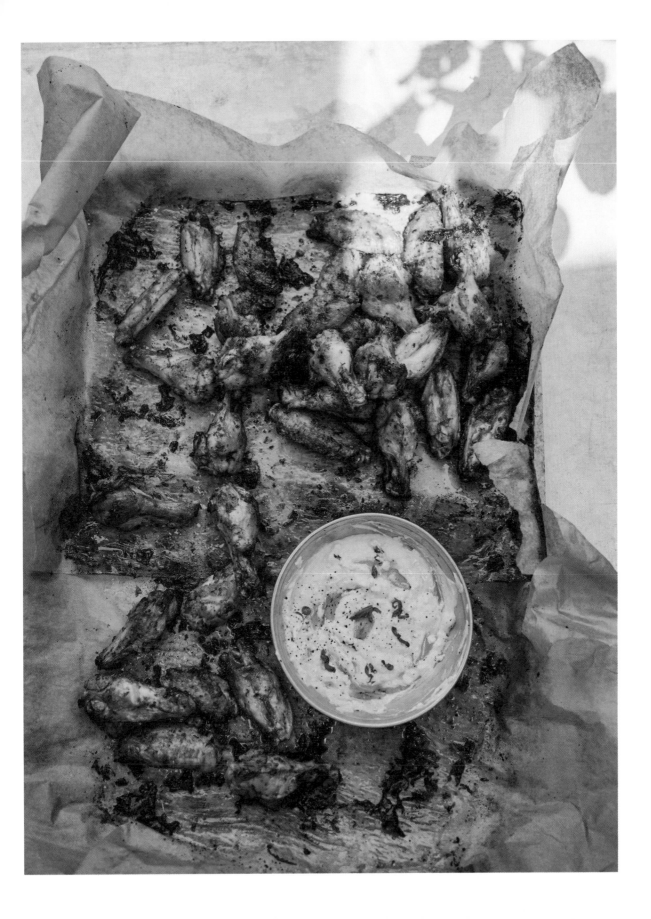

One-pot chicken thighs and rice

SERVES 4

6 large chicken thighs, skin-on
and bone-in

2 lemons, plus extra to serve
(optional)

4 tablespoons olive oil, plus a
little extra

2 teaspoons garlic powder

2 teaspoons dried oregano

2 teaspoons sea salt, plus extra
to taste

1 teaspoon freshly ground
black pepper, plus extra to taste

20g unsalted butter

75g vermicelli (or fine rice
noodles)

250g long grain rice

750ml chicken stock

2 red chillies

1 garlic clove

200g feta

150g Greek yoghurt

100g mayonnaise

40g kefalotyri or pecorino

GF

Place the chicken thighs in a large mixing bowl. Finely grate in the zest from one lemon. Squeeze in the juice, then add two tablespoons of the olive oil, the garlic powder, dried oregano, sea salt and black pepper. Toss together well, really massaging the flavours into the chicken skin. (If you can, marinate the chicken in advance, and store it covered in the fridge for a couple of hours.) When you are ready to cook the chicken, preheat your oven to 210°C/190°C fan/gas mark 6½. Take an ovenproof frying pan or flameproof casserole that's wide enough to comfortably fit the chicken and drizzle in two tablespoons of olive oil. Add the chicken thighs, skin-side down, and place on a medium heat. You want to start in a cold pan, so that the fat renders and the skin starts to turn golden. You're not cooking it through at this stage. When the skin is bronzing and starting to crisp, remove the chicken and leave, skin-side up, on a plate.

Add the butter to the pan, crush in the vermicelli and fry for 3–4 minutes, until deep golden-brown. Add the rice and stir thoroughly for a couple of minutes, so it gets coated in the butter, then pour in the chicken stock. Season generously and bring to the boil for a few minutes, then nestle in the chicken, so the meat is submerged in the stock but the skin is above the surface, so it can crisp up. Place the pan in the oven and cook for 35–40 minutes, until the rice is tender and the chicken is browned, crisp-skinned and cooked through. (Check it after about 15–20 minutes, and top up with 200ml of water if it looks like it's drying out.)

While the chicken is in the oven, make the dip. Halve, deseed and finely slice the chillies. Peel and finely slice the garlic. Place a small pan on a medium heat, add enough oil to just cover the base and fry the chillies and garlic for a minute or so, just till lightly golden, then remove from the heat. Break the feta up in a bowl and mash in the Greek yoghurt. Using a fork will be easiest; it'll be a little grainy but keep going. Stir in the mayonnaise and finely grate in the kefalotyri. Finely grate in the zest of the remaining lemon. Stir the fried chilli and garlic into the feta dip and squeeze in the juice of half of the lemon. Mix everything well. Taste and adjust the seasoning, adding more lemon, salt and pepper as needed.

Serve the chicken and rice with the dip on the side or drizzled over the top, perhaps with some lemon wedges. However you have it, it's very good.

Village pasta with chicken and lemon

GF

This is the kind of weeknight meal that makes everyone at my place go quiet. No bickering or yelling, any fractious end-of-long-day moods forgotten, just the sounds of happy munching. Golden, crunchy chicken skin is always appreciated, and the combination of lemon and halloumi makes it fresh, salty-addictive and comforting all at once. If you don't have chard, use whatever greens you do — spinach, kale, broccoli all work. Just make sure you're not shy with the halloumi — more is more.

SERVES 4

Olive oil
Sea salt and freshly ground
 black pepper
6 chicken thighs, skin-on and
 bone-in
1 teaspoon dried oregano
3 garlic cloves
400g Swiss chard
100g halloumi or salted anari, or
 to taste
1.4 litres chicken stock
250g Greek or Cypriot village
 pasta (you can use regular or
 gluten-free macaroni if needed)
1 lemon
1 tablespoon dried mint

Preheat your oven to 200°C/180°C fan/gas mark 6. Place a wide, deep flameproof casserole on a medium heat and drizzle in enough olive oil to just cover the base. Season the chicken thighs well, especially the skin, sprinkle with the dried oregano and place in the casserole skin-side down. Fry for about 10 minutes, until the skin is golden-brown, then flip over and fry for a further 10 minutes.

While the chicken is cooking, peel and finely slice the garlic. Trim the chard and shred it — stalks and all. Coarsely grate the halloumi and set aside. When the chicken is golden, remove and leave on a plate to one side. Add the garlic to the casserole and fry in the remaining oil for a couple of minutes. Add the chard and stock to the pan and bring to the boil. Stir in the pasta, bring back to the boil and cook for 5 minutes. Squeeze in the juice of the lemon and stir in half of the dried mint.

Place the chicken thighs back in the pan, skin-side up, so they sit in the pasta and place the pan in the oven. Bake for 25-30 minutes, until most of the liquid has been absorbed, the pasta is tender and the chicken is cooked and has golden-brown skin. Before serving the chicken and pasta, stir most of the grated halloumi through the pasta, and scatter the rest on top with the remaining dried mint.

Halloumi fried chicken

I have a soft spot for a breaded chicken escalope from old-school Italian sandwich bars (sadly now becoming more scarce). Would I have it in ciabatta, or with tomato spaghetti, Milanese style? Decisions, decisions. This recipe is essentially a halloumi-encrusted chicken escalope and you can eat it however you want. I like it between thick slices of fresh white bread with lettuce, lots of mayo and cucumber. Or with chips or in pita, a squeeze of lemon over the top. Other days I want it with a big twirl of garlicky tomato spaghetti, on a retro oval plate, and a sprig of parsley. Curly, of course.

SERVES 4

4 chicken breasts
75g plain flour (gluten-free,
 if needed)
Sea salt and freshly ground
 black pepper
1 large egg
80g breadcrumbs or panko
 crumbs (gluten-free, if needed)
1 ½ teaspoons dried oregano
½ teaspoon sweet smoked paprika
½ teaspoon dried mint
25g unsalted butter
Olive oil
80g halloumi, or more to taste
1 lemon, for squeezing

Place the chicken breasts between two sheets of greaseproof paper, and flatten them by hitting with a heavy pan. You want them to be even in thickness, 1.5-2cm thick. Set up a breadcrumbing station. You'll need three wide, shallow bowls — something like a pasta bowl or deep plate works best. Place the plain flour in one bowl and season well with salt and pepper. Whisk the egg in a second bowl. In a third bowl, mix the breadcrumbs with the oregano, paprika and mint, then season well. Place a large frying pan on a medium-low heat and add the butter and a drizzle of olive oil.

One at a time, coat the chicken breasts with the seasoned flour. Then dip into the egg (letting the excess drip off) and finally coat in the seasoned breadcrumbs. Place in the hot pan. Fry for 8-10 minutes on the first side. You don't want the pan too hot or the chicken will brown too quickly and won't cook through. Then turn and cook for a further 5-7 minutes. While the chicken pieces are still in the pan, finely grate over a layer of halloumi. Then flip the chicken over and fry, turning the heat up high. Grate more halloumi on the other side, and then repeat if you're a hardcore halloumi fiend. At this stage, you want to fry for just a minute or two on each side to seal the halloumi into the crust. Remove the chicken from the pan to a plate and leave to rest for a couple of minutes before serving. A squeeze of lemon over the top is very good — in fact, I'd say it's essential.

HLT kritharaki

HLT = halloumi, lountza, tomato. *The* sandwich of Cyprus (for more on that, see page 26). It's such a big part of Cypriot culture and my childhood that I wanted to pay homage again, and make it into a pasta, because... Well, just because. It's simple, unfussy, comforting and familiar. You don't have to have grown up with HLT sarnies for this to feel nostalgic.

SERVES 4

1 onion
4 garlic cloves
100g lountza or 6 rashers of
  smoked streaky bacon
½ bunch of Greek (or regular) basil
Olive oil
200g vine cherry tomatoes
2 tablespoons sun-dried tomato
  paste
300g kritharaki or orzo pasta
  (gluten-free, if needed)
Sea salt and freshly ground
  black pepper
1 × 400g tin of plum tomatoes
750ml chicken stock
1 × 250g block of halloumi
½ lemon
4 tablespoons extra virgin olive oil

Peel and finely chop the onion and three of the garlic cloves. Cut the lountza or bacon into 1cm pieces or strips. Finely chop the basil stalks, keeping the leaves to one side for later. Place a deep, wide frying pan or flameproof shallow casserole on a high heat and drizzle in a few tablespoons of olive oil. Fry the tomatoes on the vine for a few minutes until they start to blister slightly, then transfer to a plate and set aside. Reduce the heat to medium and add the chopped lountza, frying until caramelising and crisp, then stir in the chopped onion, garlic and basil stalks. Fry for 10 minutes, reducing the heat a little. Stir in the sun-dried tomato paste, then the pasta, stirring so everything is well coated. Season well, then add the tinned tomatoes, breaking them up with a wooden spoon. Stir in the stock and bring everything to the boil. Nestle in the fried vine tomatoes and cover with a lid. Reduce to a simmer and cook for 12–15 minutes, until the pasta is tender and most of the liquid has been absorbed. You'll need to give it a stir around the tomatoes a couple of times.

While the pasta is cooking, peel and roughly chop the remaining garlic clove. Chop 50g of the halloumi and place both in a blender. Add most of the basil leaves, the juice of the lemon half and the extra virgin olive oil. Season well and blitz to a smooth pesto. Cut the remaining halloumi into 1.5cm cubes.

When the pasta is cooked, make sure there is still a little liquid in the pan (if not, stir in a splash of boiling water) as it will absorb this as it cools. Remove from the heat and leave covered. Place a small frying pan on a medium-high heat, drizzle in a few tablespoons of olive oil and fry the halloumi cubes until golden and crisp on both sides — try not to turn the pieces too soon; you want it to form a golden crust and you'll only get this with good, uninterrupted heat. Ripple the basil dressing into the pasta, and garnish with the fried halloumi and remaining basil leaves.

Braised sausage, lentils and fennel

DF + GF

One-pot dinners are very much in — not just in our house but globally, it seems. We all want ease, speed and less washing up. I'm fully on board. One of my favourite Cypriot dishes has always been faki, a lentil and rice recipe, and this is essentially that but with sausages. It's a meal I make for my daughters, but one we all appreciate.

I have given a range for how many sausages you'll need to make this recipe. Supermarket sausages often come in packs of six, and that's a good number if you're feeding people of different ages. However, if your family is older, bigger or hungrier, use as many as you like.

SERVES 4

Olive oil
6–8 sausages
2 onions
4 garlic cloves
1 large or 2 small fennel bulbs
1 teaspoon fennel seeds
1 pinch of Aleppo pepper (or
  ½ teaspoon dried red chilli flakes)
1 heaped tablespoon tomato purée
150ml wine, red or white is fine
2 x 400g tins of green lentils
150ml beef or chicken stock
1 tablespoon red wine vinegar
Sea salt and freshly ground
  black pepper

Preheat your oven to 210°C/190°C fan/gas mark 6½. (You can also cook this all on the hob, if you prefer.) Place a large flameproof casserole or wide ovenproof frying pan on a medium-low heat and drizzle in a little olive oil. Fry the sausages for about 8 minutes, turning, until browned all over.

While the sausages are browning, peel and finely slice the onions and garlic. Trim the fennel, reserving any nice fronds, and cut the bulbs into wedges. Crush the fennel seeds. When the sausages are browned, remove to a plate. Add the fennel wedges to the pan and turn the heat up a little. Fry so they brown, then stir in the onions and garlic and fennel seeds. Sauté for 5 minutes, then stir in the Aleppo pepper and tomato purée. Fry, stirring, for a minute, then add the wine. Bring to the boil and simmer for a few minutes, till reduced by half, then stir in the tinned lentils, including their liquid, with the stock and red wine vinegar, and season well. Pop the browned sausages on top, bring to the boil and then cover with a lid. Transfer the pan to the oven and cook for 10 minutes. Remove the lid from the pan and cook, uncovered, for 15–20 minutes, until everything is nicely browned and the lentils are thickened. Serve scattered with the reserved fennel fronds.

One-pan pastitsio

GF

When I started writing this book, I set myself a challenge: to make much-loved Greek dishes more achievable. To be fair, a lot of our recipes are pretty straightforward, but one request that came up time and again is pastitsio (or as Cypriots call it, makaronia tou fournou). Pastitsio isn't particularly tricky, but it is laborious. There's the slow-cooked ragu, the cooked pasta, and then a béchamel. How can we strip this back? By making the whole thing using only one pan. You read that right. One. Pan. Ragu, pasta and sauce. Of course, it's not the same as classic pastitsio in terms of layers and drama. But I think it has its own dramatic appeal; the whole thing is cooked in a large frying pan and that looks pretty epic.

SERVES 4

Olive oil

500g mince — ideally beef, perhaps some pork too

Sea salt and freshly ground black pepper

2 onions

4 garlic cloves

1 teaspoon dried oregano, plus a pinch

½ teaspoon ground cinnamon

2 tablespoons tomato purée

250g pastitsio pasta, bucatini or even penne (gluten-free, if needed)

1 litre beef stock

300ml crème fraîche

2 egg yolks

100g graviera, kefalotyri or pecorino

You'll need a wide, deep frying pan for this dish. If you don't have one you confidently think will fit all the ingredients, make it in a large saucepan. Place your pan on a high heat and drizzle in a good few tablespoons of olive oil. Add the mince to the pan, and break it up well with a wooden spoon. Season generously, and fry for 5-8 minutes, so that any liquid evaporates and the mince starts to crisp. Meanwhile, peel and finely chop the onions and garlic. When the mince has started to brown, stir them in with the oregano and cinnamon. Fry for a further 5 minutes, reducing the heat a little, stirring everything together (add a touch extra olive oil if it looks dry). Stir in the tomato purée, fry off for a minute or two, then add the pasta to the pan. If you are using traditional pastitsio pasta or bucatini you may need to snap some of the pieces in half to fit them all in. It'll be snug in the pan, but try to fit them all. Pour over the beef stock, season and bring to the boil. Cover the pan, reduce the heat to low and simmer for 20 minutes, stirring once or twice.

While the pasta is cooking, mix together the crème fraîche and egg yolks. Finely grate the cheese and stir in most of it with a generous pinch of salt and pepper. When your pasta is ready, turn your grill to high. Gently toss the pasta and sauce in the pan together. Spoon the crème fraîche mixture over the top and sprinkle with the remaining grated cheese, plus an additional pinch of dried oregano. Place under the grill, not too close to the bars, and grill for 3-5 minutes, until golden and bubbling on top. Keep an eye on it, as how long it takes will depend on the strength of your grill. Remove and leave to stand for at least 5-10 minutes before serving.

Classic biftekia and chips

Biftekia are the Greek version of beef burgers, but instead of being served in a bun, they're baked in a tray with potato wedges and the classic lemon-oregano dressing. That's not to say you can't shove one of these in a bun — there are times that I certainly do — but this is a good one-tray dinner. I've kept this recipe traditional, but have a play: a little dried red chilli in the mince, some slices of cheese on top for the last few minutes in the oven... Make this your own. Perhaps add a gesture of a salad on the side for good manners.

SERVES 4

400g beef mince
2 garlic cloves
1 red onion
1 ripe tomato
2 ½ teaspoons dried oregano
1 teaspoon dried mint
25g dried breadcrumbs
 (gluten-free, if needed)
75ml whole milk (or plant-based,
 if needed)
1 bunch of flat-leaf parsley
1 large egg
Sea salt and freshly ground
 black pepper
Olive oil
3 baking or large waxy potatoes
 (about 600g)
1 lemon

Preheat your oven to 200°C/180°C fan/gas mark 6. Place the beef mince in a large mixing bowl. Finely grate in one garlic clove. Coarsely grate in the peeled onion and the tomato, discarding the tomato skin. Add two teaspoons of the dried oregano, the dried mint, breadcrumbs and the milk. Finely chop the parsley and add half to the bowl. Crack in the egg and season generously. Drizzle in a couple of tablespoons of olive oil and scrunch everything together really well, so it's well mixed.

Cut the potatoes into 2.5cm-thick wedges. Place in a large roasting tray and finely grate in the zest of the lemon and the remaining garlic clove. Sprinkle over the remaining ½ teaspoon of the dried oregano, season generously and squeeze over the juice of the lemon. Toss everything together well, then pour a couple of tablespoons of water into the base of the tray. Divide the mince into four equal patties — you want to flatten them out quite a bit as they will shrink in the oven. Nestle the burgers in among the potatoes, and drizzle over a final bit of olive oil.

Cover the tray tightly with foil and pop in the oven for 10 minutes. Remove the foil and continue to cook for a further 30-35 minutes, until the potatoes are golden and the biftekia are well crusted and cooked through. Finish by scattering over the remaining parsley. These are great as they are but also delicious in a bun with cheese, the Western way.

Little lamb meatballs with chickpeas

DF + GF

I love this recipe; it is quietly pleasurable to make — rolling out the little meatballs — and also comforting to eat. It's proper unfussy hearty food, and perfect with steaming pilafi (page 211) and a dollop of the tangiest Greek yoghurt you can get your hands on.

SERVES 4

½ bunch of mint
3 red onions
3 garlic cloves
½ bunch of flat-leaf parsley
Sea salt and freshly ground
 black pepper
50g breadcrumbs (gluten-free,
 if needed)
1 teaspoon sweet smoked paprika
½ teaspoon dried mint
1 lemon
500g lamb mince
Olive oil
1 tablespoon plain flour
 (gluten-free, if needed)
2 tablespoons tomato purée
2 × 400g tins of chickpeas or
 1 × 700g jar
300ml beef stock

Pick the mint leaves. Peel and chop one red onion and two garlic cloves. Place in a food processor with the flat-leaf parsley, stalks and all, and half the mint leaves. Pulse until finely chopped, then season well, add the breadcrumbs, paprika and dried mint. Finely grate in the lemon zest. Pulse, then add the lamb mince. Pulse a few more times, until it all just comes together. Transfer to a bowl, mix and scrunch together a little more with your hands and then roll into little meatballs, about 2.5cm wide. To make it easier, you can rub your hands with a little oil or water first.

Peel and finely chop the remaining onions and garlic. Place a large frying pan on a medium heat, drizzle in a little olive oil and fry the meatballs for about 5 minutes, until browned all over. Add the chopped onions and garlic, reduce the heat a little and sauté for a further 10 minutes. Sprinkle in the plain flour and stir until everything is coated. After a minute, stir in the tomato purée. Fry for a couple more minutes, then add the chickpeas, liquid and all, and the stock. If you've used jarred chickpeas, you may need to add a little more water. Season generously, bring to the boil, then reduce the heat a little and simmer, gently bubbling away for 15–20 minutes. If it still looks liquidy, let it simmer for a little longer. Finely shred or tear the remaining mint leaves, then sprinkle over. Serve as is, or with fresh bread or pilafi and tangy Greek yoghurt (dairy-free, if you prefer).

Spiced lamb chops with houmous

In terms of instant dinner gratification, you can't get much better than this. It's up there as one of the quickest meals in the book, worthy to make any weekly repertoire. It takes such little effort for such a lot of flavour — especially if you buy good ready-made houmous. You can of course make your own: follow the recipe on page 78, but omit the artichokes.

SERVES 4

8 lamb chops
2 garlic cloves
Sea salt and freshly ground
  black pepper
1 teaspoon ground cumin
1 teaspoon ground coriander
Olive oil
2 lemons
2 shallots
2 green chillies
A few sprigs of mint
30g pistachios or almonds
200g houmous, shop-bought or
  homemade (see page 78, just
  leave out the grilled artichokes)

Place the lamb chops in a mixing bowl or dish and crush in the garlic. Season well and add the ground cumin and coriander. Pour in enough olive oil to coat and squeeze in the juice of one lemon. Really massage the flavours into the chops, then cover and leave to marinate in the fridge for as long as you can, bringing it out 20 minutes before you want to cook. If you don't have much time, just leave to one side on the kitchen counter for at least 5 minutes.

While the lamb is marinating, peel and finely slice the shallots. Place in a small bowl with the juice of the remaining lemon and a good pinch of salt. Halve, deseed and finely slice the chillies. Toss through the lemony shallots. Pick the mint leaves and roughly chop. Finely chop the nuts, then set aside. Spoon the houmous out on a serving plate.

Place a griddle pan on a high heat and get it hot. Grill the lamb chops for about 4 minutes on each side — this will give you just-blushing lamb. You can cook them for less or more time depending on your taste. I like to finish by propping them up on the fatty side to get it crisp (this was always my mum's favourite bit). You don't want to crowd the pan, so you might need to do this in two batches; if so, rest the cooked chops in a very low oven while you cook the others. As soon as all the chops are ready, place them on top of the houmous. Toss the mint through the shallot mixture and scatter over the top with the nuts.

Charred oyster mushrooms, mustard and thyme
Halloumi, tomato and honey kebabs
Prawn saganaki kebabs
Saffron and fennel fish kebabs with caper mayo
Spiced chilli and coriander chicken
Classic pork with oregano
Lamb and halloumi kofta

Extras

Golden mustard sauce
Crispy garlic oven chips
Chopped kebab salad

Things on sticks

Charred oyster mushrooms, mustard and thyme

I like to rank food in Top Five lists. (We all do it, yeah?) At the time of writing, this is in my top two skewers. It's easy and nutritious and don't only think of it as a vegan offering — I tell you from experience, carnivores will bite your hand off for one.

MAKES 4 SKEWERS

250g oyster mushrooms
½ bunch of thyme
1 garlic clove
3 tablespoons olive oil
1 tablespoon Dijon mustard
Sea salt and freshly ground
 black pepper
1 lemon
A few sprigs of flat-leaf parsley

Wipe the mushrooms clean. Make the marinade in a large mixing bowl. Pick in the thyme leaves. Peel and finely grate in the garlic. Add the olive oil, the Dijon mustard, a good pinch of salt and pepper and then squeeze in the lemon juice. Whisk together and then toss in the mushrooms. Really massage the flavours into them. Leave to marinate for 30 minutes, if you have time (or in the fridge for longer).

When you are ready to grill, divide the mushrooms between four skewers (if using bamboo be sure to soak in cold water for half an hour first). Push the mushrooms along the skewer, not too close together, so they have a chance to char nicely. Place the skewers directly on a hot barbecue or griddle pan. Grill for 3-4 minutes on each side, until golden-brown and crisp at the edges; do not turn them more than once — let them char. Finely chop the parsley and sprinkle over the cooked skewers, then serve immediately.

VG + GF

Halloumi, tomato and honey kebabs

V + GF

You're a vegetarian at a barbecue? If you're eating with my family, you're not an afterthought. We don't do sad, unseasoned veg kebabs. Although I think that halloumi is perfection in its own right, I do occasionally like to jazz it up. As halloumi is often made with a sprinkling of mint, this simple marinade complements rather than overpowers, and the tomatoes add a touch of sweetness and softness. Nothing second best here.

MAKES 4

2 tablespoons olive oil
1 tablespoon white wine vinegar
½ teaspoon Aleppo pepper (or
  ¼ teaspoon dried red chilli flakes)
1 teaspoon dried oregano
½ teaspoon dried mint
2 garlic cloves
1 × 250g block of halloumi
12 cherry tomatoes (about 150g)
A few sprigs of mint
4 tablespoons honey

In a large mixing bowl, whisk together the olive oil, white wine vinegar, Aleppo pepper, dried oregano and dried mint. Peel and finely grate in the garlic. Cut the halloumi into 16 even pieces. Toss through the marinade, cover the bowl and leave to marinate for half an hour. (Or in the fridge for longer.) Soak your skewers, if using bamboo ones.

Get your barbecue or griddle pan hot. Toss the tomatoes through the halloumi pieces so they get a bit of the marinade on them. Thread four pieces of halloumi on each skewer, with a cherry tomato in between each piece. Pick and finely slice the mint leaves. On a hot barbecue or griddle pan, grill each skewer for 3–4 minutes on each side, until charred and softened, drizzling each skewer with a tablespoon of honey for the last couple of minutes. Serve sprinkled with the mint leaves.

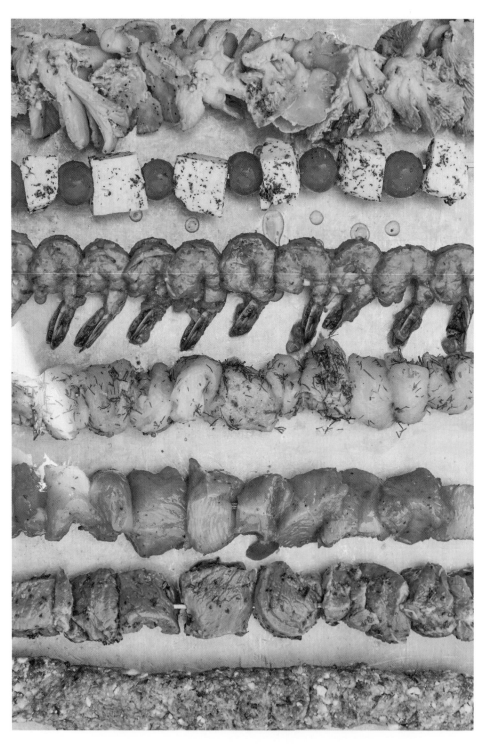

Kebabs from top: charred oyster mushrooms, mustard and thyme (page 134); halloumi, tomato and honey (page 135); prawn saganaki (page 138); saffron and fennel fish (page 139); spiced chilli and coriander chicken (page 142); classic pork with oregano (page 143); lamb and halloumi kofta (page 144)

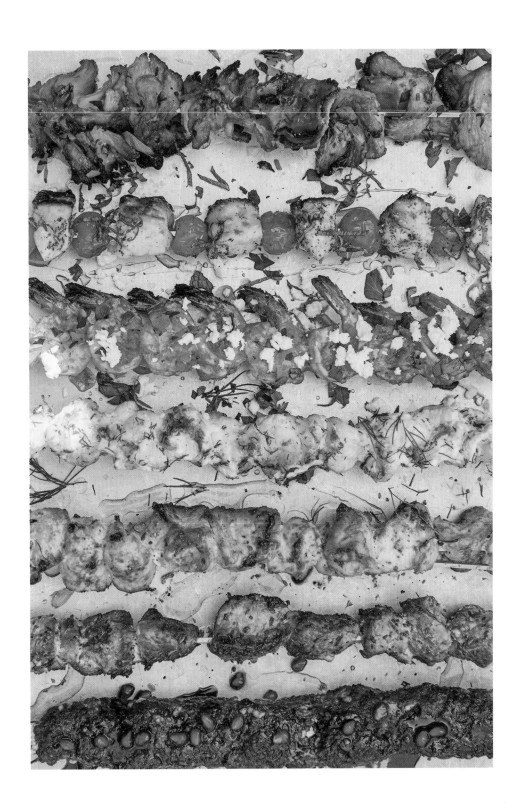

Prawn saganaki kebabs

Prawn saganaki is a recipe that my family and I love, and I would say successfully busts the myth that you can't serve seafood and cheese. (Who makes these rules? Fools.) This recipe takes the prawns and feta out of the traditional pan (the saganaki) and I think is the best way to make a prawn skewer. Use lovely fat king prawns, leave the tails on if you can, and marinate them for as long as possible. Crucially, serve the skewers with extra lemon for squeezing over and bread for mopping up all the juices.

MAKES 4 SKEWERS

2 ripe tomatoes
2 garlic cloves
4 tablespoons olive oil
1 teaspoon Aleppo pepper (or
  ½ teaspoon dried red chilli flakes)
1 teaspoon dried oregano
75ml ouzo (optional)
½ teaspoon caster sugar
Sea salt and freshly ground
  black pepper
24 large king prawns (see intro)
½ bunch of flat-leaf parsley
100g feta
1 lemon

Coarsely grate the tomatoes on a box grater and discard the skins. Peel and finely chop the garlic. Place a medium pan on a low heat and drizzle in the olive oil. Add the garlic and fry for a minute. Add the Aleppo pepper and dried oregano, then pour in the ouzo, if using. Turn up the heat and reduce the ouzo by half. Be careful, as the ouzo will probably catch alight — that is OK, the alcohol will burn off quickly, but don't leave the pan unattended. When it has reduced, add the grated tomatoes with the caster sugar and a generous pinch each of sea salt and black pepper. Bring back to the boil and cook for a further 10 minutes, until thickened slightly. Leave to cool completely.

Place the prawns in a mixing bowl or sealed container and stir in the cooled tomato sauce. Cover and leave to marinate in the fridge for at least 1 hour (the longer the better). If using bamboo skewers, make sure you soak them in water first for at least half an hour to stop them burning.

You can cook these on a hot griddle pan or under a hot grill but they're best done on a barbecue. When you're ready to cook, thread six prawns on each skewer, but don't push them too close together. Baste the skewers with the remaining mixture in the bowl, and cook for a couple of minutes on each side until charred and pink. Finely chop the parsley, and transfer the skewers to a platter. Scatter over the parsley, crumble over the feta and squeeze over the lemon juice.

Saffron and fennel fish kebabs with caper mayo

One of the biggest differences between Greek and Cypriot cuisine is dill versus coriander. For Cypriots, one of the strongest flavour profiles is coriander (whether in seed form or fresh leaf) with lemon. In Greece, there is a liberal use of dill, and it is a flavour I have grown to adore. For meat kebabs, I more often go with the warmer spice of coriander seed, but with firm white fish, I choose the Greek way of less spice more herbs.

MAKES 4 SKEWERS

A pinch of saffron
½ teaspoon fennel seeds
1 lemon
½ bunch of dill
500g firm white fish, such as
  monkfish
3 tablespoons olive oil, plus
  a little extra
Sea salt and freshly ground
  black pepper
4 tablespoons mayonnaise
1½ tablespoons capers

Place the saffron in a large mixing bowl and top with 75ml of just-boiled water. Leave to cool. Grind the fennel seeds. Place in the mixing bowl and finely grate in the lemon zest. Finely chop the dill and add half of it to the saffron mixture. Cut the fish into even pieces, about 2.5cm, and stir into the cooled marinade. Drizzle with the olive oil and mix together well. Cover and leave in the fridge for at least 30 minutes, but longer if you can. If you're using bamboo skewers, soak four of them for 30 minutes.

When you are ready to cook the monkfish, season the fish generously. Thread equally on the skewers, but don't push too close together or they won't cook evenly. Rub in a little more olive oil. Place the skewers on the hot barbecue bars or on a hot griddle pan and cook for about 6-8 minutes, turning halfway through, until charred and cooked through.

Meanwhile, stir the remaining chopped dill into the mayonnaise with the capers and the juice of half the lemon. Season to taste. Serve the skewers with the caper mayo and the remaining lemon cut into wedges.

GF

Spiced chilli and coriander chicken

GF

I mentioned that the oyster mushroom skewer (page 134) was in my current top two on the kebab charts — it's fighting for the top spot with this bad boy. This recipe is simple, perfectly spiced and if you like chicken, you'll love it.

MAKES 4 SKEWERS

500g chicken breast
4 garlic cloves
50g unsalted butter
1 teaspoon ground coriander
½ teaspoon ground cumin
1 teaspoon Aleppo pepper (or
 ½ teaspoon dried chilli flakes)
Sea salt and freshly ground
 black pepper
2 tablespoons olive oil

Trim the chicken and cut into even-sized pieces, about 2.5cm big. Peel and finely chop the garlic. Melt the butter and place in a mixing bowl or non-reactive container with a lid. Stir in the chopped garlic, ground coriander, ground cumin and Aleppo pepper. Season generously with sea salt and black pepper. Stir in the olive oil. When the mixture is room temperature, stir in the chicken pieces. Mix together well and cover or seal. Pop in the fridge for at least 1 hour — if you can, overnight will make a huge difference.

If you are using bamboo skewers, make sure you soak them in water first for at least 30 minutes to stop them burning. Evenly divide the meat between the skewers, making sure they're not pushed too close together. Then barbecue or cook in a hot griddle pan for about 10–12 minutes, until charred and just cooked through (you can test one piece by making sure it isn't pink in the middle). Serve straight away.

Classic pork with oregano

This one needs no introduction. I'm not reinventing the wheel here, but you can't mess or go wrong with a classic pork souvlaki.

MAKES 4 SKEWERS

500g pork neck or shoulder, or
  even tenderloin
A few sprigs of rosemary
1 teaspoon dried oregano, plus
  extra to serve
1 garlic clove
Sea salt and freshly ground
  black pepper
4 tablespoons olive oil
1 tablespoon red wine vinegar
1 lemon, to serve

Cut the pork into even 2.5cm chunks and place in a mixing bowl. Pick and finely chop the rosemary and add to the pork with the dried oregano. Peel and finely grate in the garlic. Season well and stir in the olive oil and red wine vinegar and cover. Refrigerate and leave to marinate for at least half an hour, more if possible. If using bamboo skewers, be sure to soak them in water first for 30 minutes to stop them burning.

When you are ready to cook, divide the pork between four skewers. Be careful not to push the pieces too close together, so that they cook thoroughly all the way through. Cook the meat on a hot griddle pan or barbecue for about 10-12 minutes, turning evenly, until they are charred and cooked through. Be sure to finish with lots of lemon squeezed over the top and extra dried oregano sprinkled over.

Lamb and halloumi kofta

This is a lovely little number; simple but effective. The tanginess from the pomegranate and salty halloumi play so nicely against that fattiness from lamb mince. If you're feeling super snazzy, sprinkle with some fresh pomegranate seeds at the end.

MAKES 8 SMALL SKEWERS

400g lamb mince
½ red onion
1 teaspoon ground cumin
1 teaspoon ground coriander
½ teaspoon ground cinnamon
Sea salt and freshly ground
 black pepper
½ bunch of flat-leaf parsley
50g halloumi
Olive oil
1½ tablespoons pomegranate
 molasses
Pomegranate seeds, to serve
 (optional)

Place the lamb mince in a mixing bowl. Coarsely grate the red onion and add to the bowl with the ground cumin, coriander and cinnamon, then season generously. Finely chop the flat-leaf parsley and add most of it to the mince mixture. Scrunch everything together really well. At the end, coarsely grate in the halloumi and work a little more to distribute. Divide the mixture between eight skewers (if using bamboo skewers, be sure to soak them for 30 minutes first) and scrunch around the skewers so you have long, oval, slightly flattened kofta, using your fingers to make indents along the flattened edges.

Check your barbecue is ready, or place a griddle pan on a high heat (or you can use a frying pan). Rub the kofta with olive oil and grill or fry for 3 minutes on one side, and then turn and cook for 2 minutes on the other. They will smoke, but will get a lovely charred crust. Finish with a drizzle of pomegranate molasses, the remaining chopped parsley and, if you like, a scattering of pomegranate seeds.

Golden mustard sauce

SERVES 4

50g Greek yoghurt
3 tablespoons mayonnaise
2–3 tablespoons English mustard
1–2 tablespoons honey

Mix together the Greek yoghurt, mayonnaise and two tablespoons of English mustard with one tablespoon of honey. Taste, and adjust the heat and sweetness, adding a little more mustard and honey to your taste.

Crispy garlic oven chips

SERVES 4

750g baking potatoes
Olive oil
2 teaspoons garlic powder
Sea salt and freshly ground
 black pepper

Preheat your oven to 200°C/180°C fan/gas mark 6. Wash and dry the potatoes, then cut into 1–1.5cm-thick chips — leave the skin on. Place the chips on a large baking tray, drizzle with a couple of tablespoons of olive oil and sprinkle over the garlic powder. Season generously and toss to combine. Really rub everything into the chips. Spread out in a single layer, and cook for 25 minutes — don't touch them. After that time, turn them over and return to the oven for a further 5–10 minutes, until they're crisp and deep golden all over.

Chopped kebab salad

SERVES 4

1 onion
¼ white cabbage
Sea salt and freshly ground
 black pepper
1 lemon
2 tomatoes
½ cucumber
½ bunch flat-leaf parsley
Extra virgin olive oil

Peel, halve and finely slice the onion. Shred the cabbage as finely as you can. Place both in a large mixing bowl, season generously with sea salt and black pepper and squeeze over the lemon juice. Scrunch everything together and leave for 5 minutes. Meanwhile, cut the tomatoes into small bite-sized pieces. Halve the cucumber lengthwise and slice into thin half-moons. Finely chop the parsley. Toss the tomatoes, cucumber and parsley through the cabbage, then stir in a couple of tablespoons of extra virgin olive oil. Taste, adjust the seasoning and serve alongside any kebab.

Vegetables

Hasselback imam bayildi
Green gigantes: caramelised onion, leek and courgette
  butter beans
Whole roast cabbage with spiced butter
Pumpkin and feta kataifi pie

Fish

Psari plaki: baked fish with tomatoes and olives
Lemon and herb salt-baked bream
Psarosoupa: golden fish soup

Meat

Tserepa: roast chicken, potatoes and peppers
Roast chicken with tomatoey bulgur wheat
Pulled chicken gyro with all the trimmings
Pork shoulder, beans and chard
Triple-fennel pork belly
Youvesti: my favourite meat and orzo stew
Pastitsada: spiced beef with pasta
Kreatopites: little meat pies
Lamb shank fricassee with preserved lemon
Slow-roasted 30 garlic lamb shoulder

Feasts

Hasselback imam bayildi

VG + GF

This Turkish dish is loved throughout Greece and is considered to be *politiki kouzina*, meaning 'food of the city'. The city in question is Constantinople, now Istanbul, the heart of the Greek-speaking world for many years. There are many politiki kouzina recipes, but imam bayildi is the most famous. Translated from Turkish, the name means 'the imam fainted'. It's said this was due to the deliciousness of the dish, which I think is fair. I would swoon if someone made this for me. Another theory is that the imam fainted over the cost when he heard how much olive oil was used; that's probably fair, too. I'm conservative with my oil use, but it is necessary to use a bit for the most flavoursome aubergines. In most recipes, the aubergines are cooked whole, then split open. Cutting them in this way, like hasselback potatoes, is something that I've only ever seen my yiayia do. I love it.

SERVES 4

2 onions
4 garlic cloves
½ bunch of flat-leaf parsley
About 125ml olive oil
Sea salt and freshly ground
 black pepper
1½ teaspoons dried oregano
1 teaspoon sweet smoked paprika
1 teaspoon ground cumin
½ teaspoon ground coriander
1 heaped tablespoon tomato purée
1 x 400g tin of plum tomatoes
2 large aubergines
1 x 200g block of feta (optional)

Peel and finely chop the onions and two garlic cloves. Peel and finely slice the remaining two cloves. Finely chop the parsley stalks and leaves; keep them separate. Place a large, deep ovenproof frying pan on a medium-low heat and add four tablespoons of olive oil, then the onions, chopped garlic and parsley stalks. Season, then soften for 10 minutes. Stir in the oregano, paprika, cumin and coriander. After a few minutes, stir in the tomato purée. After a further few minutes, stir in the tin of tomatoes and a tin of water. Turn up the heat, break up the tomatoes and bring to the boil. Once it's bubbling, season again, reduce the heat and simmer for 10 minutes.

Preheat your oven to 200°C/180°C fan/gas mark 6. Slice the aubergines in 1cm widths (see photo), but don't slice all the way through. You can spear a skewer through the length of the aubergine, about two-thirds down, or place the aubergine between wooden spoons. This will stop you cutting all the way through. Slightly fan out the slices and generously season between the cuts and on top. Rub each aubergine with a couple of tablespoons of olive oil, really getting into the cuts, and dot the sliced garlic into the grooves.

When the sauce has thickened, stir in half the parsley leaves. Nestle in the aubergines, spooning the sauce over the top. Cover with a lid and bake for 1 hour. Remove the lid, drizzle with a little more oil and bake uncovered for 20-25 minutes, until the aubergines are tender and the sauce is thickened. Roughly break or slice the feta, if using, and push a piece in between each aubergine slice. Scatter with the remaining parsley and serve. This is dreamy warm, but even better at room temperature.

Green gigantes: *caramelised onion, leek and courgette butter beans*

This simple dish is a riff on the much-loved gigantes, an iconic Greek meal featuring giant butter beans. I love the tomatoey original, but this green version is as delicious. It feels light rather than rich and hearty, though it is substantial enough to be a standalone meal, perhaps with bread and pickles on the side. It is also much better when it is made in advance; I very much recommend that you double the recipe and eat it over a few days.

SERVES 4

2 onions
2 garlic cloves
2 leeks
2 courgettes
6 tablespoons olive oil
A few sprigs of thyme
Sea salt and freshly ground
   black pepper
1 teaspoon caster sugar
1 tablespoon sweet smoked
   paprika
2 × 400g tins of butter beans

Preheat your oven to 210°C/190°C fan/gas mark 6½. Peel and finely slice the onions and then the garlic. Trim and finely slice the leeks and courgettes — I like to slice my courgettes into half-moons. Give the leeks a really good rinse. Place a flameproof casserole on a medium-low heat and add the olive oil and all the sliced vegetables. Pick in the thyme leaves. Season generously with salt and pepper, stir in the caster sugar and cook for 30 minutes, until softened and golden. Stir everything occasionally and if the mixture starts to catch on the bottom, add a little splash of water. Stir in the sweet smoked paprika for the final 10 minutes of cooking.

When the vegetables are golden, stir in the beans, including the liquid from the tins, and top with an extra 200ml of water. Bring to the boil, then place the uncovered casserole in the oven for about an hour (if you are doubling the recipe, cook for an extra 30 minutes). Check the beans a couple of times during cooking to make sure they aren't drying out — if they are, add a splash more water. The end result should be golden and a little crisped on top with oozy beans underneath. I like to leave this to cool for a little while before serving.

Whole roast cabbage with spiced butter

VG + GF

Every time I visit Cyprus during the winter months I'm delighted by the abundance of fresh produce. A trip to Aunt Frosa and Uncle George's allotment yielded portobello mushrooms bigger than my head and the biggest cabbage I have ever seen. It fascinates me that cabbage often gets a bad rap, as it's one of my favourite vegetables, and we use it in a real range of ways — from soups and slaws, to stuffing the leaves. In this recipe, an underrated ingredient becomes a worthy hero. It's a great slow-cook recipe that you can happily forget about. If you want to use a plant-based butter for a vegan meal, that would work too. Serve with fluffy rice or pilafi (page 211) or with a side of potatoes.

SERVES 4-6

4 garlic cloves
1 lemon
1 tablespoon sweet smoked
 paprika
1 teaspoon ground coriander
½ teaspoon Aleppo pepper (or
 ¼ teaspoon dried red chilli flakes)
100g unsalted butter (dairy-free, if
 needed), at room temperature
Sea salt and freshly ground
 black pepper
4 onions
1 white cabbage (about 750g)
500ml hot vegetable stock
Olive oil

Preheat your oven to 200°C/180°C fan/gas mark 6. Peel the garlic and finely grate into a small bowl. Finely grate in the lemon zest. Add the sweet smoked paprika, ground coriander and Aleppo pepper. Chop and add in the unsalted butter and beat together with a good pinch of sea salt and black pepper.

Peel and cut the onions into 2.5cm wedges. Slice the base off the cabbage and, as carefully as you can, use a sharp paring knife to hollow out and remove some of the core. Sit the cabbage upside down in a deep ovenproof casserole or a roasting tin, so the hollowed-out core is facing up. Scatter the onion wedges around it. Spoon a third of the butter into the hollowed-out core, then dot a further third around the onions and cabbage. Pour the hot stock into the base of the tray. Drizzle everything with olive oil and season with a little salt and pepper.

Cover with the lid or tightly with foil and place in the oven for 1 hour and 15 minutes. Remove the tray from the oven, and uncover. Carefully turn the cabbage over, so it is core-side down. Pierce the top a few times with a sharp knife and baste with the remaining butter. Squeeze the juice of half the lemon into the onions and return the tray to the oven for a further hour, until everything is tender and slightly charred. Serve wedges of the cabbage with ladlefuls of soft onions and spiced, buttery juices.

Pumpkin and feta kataifi pie

V

This is a descendant of my courgette pie from *Taverna*, which (and I don't mean to boast) has been a hit far and wide. I love how thrown together it is for something that is encased in pastry. You don't need to be a perfectionist, or too scientific about anything. It is creamy, cheesy and very good. Especially with a punchy salad or as part of a large spread.

SERVES 8

600g peeled butternut squash
 or pumpkin
Olive oil
¼ teaspoon ground cinnamon
½ teaspoon ground coriander
½ teaspoon Aleppo pepper (or
 ¼ teaspoon dried red chilli flakes)
Sea salt and freshly ground black
 pepper
A large knob of butter
200g feta
200g kasseri or gruyère (or even
 cheddar)
½ bunch of spring onions
½ bunch of coriander (or
 flat-leaf parsley)
4 large eggs
300g kataifi pastry
400ml whole milk
300ml double cream
3 tablespoons honey
3 tablespoons dukkah

Preheat your oven to 200°C/180°C fan/gas mark 6. Peel the butternut squash or pumpkin and cut into small pieces, about 1.5cm wide. Place in a 30cm × 20cm roasting tin with sides and drizzle with olive oil. Sprinkle over the cinnamon, coriander and Aleppo pepper. Season well, toss together and roast for 30 minutes. When the squash is ready, transfer to a large bowl, and turn the oven off. Wipe the tray a little, then grease with butter and set aside.

Crumble the feta into the squash and coarsely grate in the other cheese. Trim and finely slice the spring onions. Finely chop the herbs and add both to the bowl. Crack in one of the eggs. Add one teaspoon of black pepper and whisk it all together.

Tease a little more than half the kataifi pastry into the greased tray, so that it covers the base evenly and comes slightly up the sides. Fill with the cheese-squash mixture, then drape over the remaining pastry so the filling is encased. Whisk the remaining eggs with the milk and cream, then pour evenly over the entire pie. Leave to one side for 30 minutes, preheating your oven to 200°C/180°C fan/gas mark 6 towards the end.

Drizzle the top of the pie with olive oil and bake for 30 minutes. Remove from the oven, drizzle over the honey and scatter over the dukkah, then return to the oven for 5-10 more minutes, until deep golden-brown and crisp on top. Leave in the tray for at least 10 minutes before serving.

Psari plaki:
baked fish with tomatoes and olives

I love how literal the naming process is with Greek dishes: *psari plaki* translates as 'baked fish'. As well as fish, there are always cooked-down tomatoes and a generous helping of olive oil, plus a range of flavour accents. I was torn on where to include this recipe; it could have gone in the weeknight chapter, as it isn't particularly laborious. Yet it is quite impressive, in the way that well-cooked fish often is. I'll leave the setting and situation up to you. It's fancy yet casual and great any night of the week.

SERVES 4

2 red onions

4 garlic cloves

5 tablespoons olive oil

Sea salt and freshly ground
 black pepper

2 teaspoons dried oregano

½ teaspoon Aleppo pepper (or
 ¼ teaspoon dried red chilli flakes)

1 × 400g tin tomatoes or passata

½ bunch of flat-leaf parsley

2 tablespoons capers

60g pitted black olives

600g white fish, such as cod
 or haddock

½ teaspoon ground cumin

1 lemon

Preheat your oven to 200°C/180°C fan/gas mark 6. Peel and finely slice the onions and garlic. Place a large ovenproof frying pan or shallow flameproof casserole on a medium-low heat and add the olive oil, onions and garlic. Season well and sauté for 10 minutes so they start to soften. Stir in one and a half teaspoons of dried oregano and all the Aleppo pepper, followed by the tinned tomatoes and 100ml of water. Break the tomatoes up with a spoon and bring everything to the boil. Reduce the heat and simmer for 15 minutes, until thickened. Finely chop the flat-leaf parsley and then stir in most of it, along with all the capers. Roughly chop and add the black olives.

If your fish is in one piece, cut into four equal portions. Pat the fish dry and place in a non-reactive bowl or dish. Season it well and sprinkle with the cumin and remaining ½ teaspoon of oregano. Squeeze over the juice of half a lemon and toss it all together. Nestle the fish in the tomato sauce. Place the pan in the oven and bake for about 20–25 minutes. How long this takes will depend on the thickness of your fish. To test it is done, check that the fish flakes easily when you insert the tip of a knife into the middle of a fillet. Finish by squeezing over the remaining lemon half and sprinkling with the remaining chopped parsley.

Lemon and herb salt-baked bream

This is another dish that is very simple but feels celebratory. It has a real sense of drama about it, as you lift off the crisp, golden salt crust to reveal the most tender and flavoursome fish. This, with a little herby yoghurt or mayo on the side and some simple salads, is my idea of pure luxury.

SERVES 4

2kg coarse sea salt

4 large egg whites

2 tablespoons fennel seeds

1 tablespoon coriander seeds

2 lemons

1 fennel bulb

4 sea bream or bass, gutted and cleaned (not scaled)

1 bunch of flat-leaf parsley

A few sprigs of oregano

1 garlic clove

250g Greek yoghurt (dairy free, if needed)

Olive oil

Sea salt and freshly ground black pepper

Preheat your oven to 200°C/180°C fan/gas mark 6. Place the sea salt in a large mixing bowl and add the egg whites, fennel seeds and coriander seeds. Finely grate in the lemon zest and add a few tablespoons of water – just enough to bring it all together. Line a large roasting tray with greaseproof paper, then pat in just under half of the sea salt mixture (if you don't have a large tray you can do this on two smaller ones).

Finely slice one of the lemons and the fennel. Stuff the cavities of the fish with both, along with a few sprigs of the flat-leaf parsley. Place the fish on the salt base and then top with the remaining sea salt mixture, really making sure they're completely covered. Place the tray in the oven for 30 minutes, and bake. To check the fish are ready, insert a skewer into the middle of one for a few seconds then touch it; it should be hot.

Meanwhile, make the herb yoghurt. Place the remaining parsley in a food processor and pick in the oregano leaves. Peel and roughly chop the garlic and add along with the juice of the remaining lemon. Blitz with half of the yoghurt until smooth; transfer to a bowl and stir in the remaining yoghurt and a few tablespoons of olive oil, then season to taste.

When the fish is ready, gently crack away the salt casing and carefully pull it away from the fish and discard. Brush away any loose salt and remove the skin also. Flake the meat from the bone in large pieces and transfer to your serving plates or platter. Serve with the herby yoghurt on the side.

Psarosoupa: *golden fish soup*

DF + GF

In English, 'fish soup' doesn't sound particularly sexy. Greek 'psarosoupa' is mysterious and alluring, and somehow promises so much more. This version is gently spiced, with lots of flavour and sweetness coming from the attention you give the base. The fish is easily adjustable to whatever is fresh and available to you. If you switch it up, you might need to adjust the cooking time, although once it's chopped up, no seafood should take a particularly long time, so always add it towards the end of cooking.

SERVES 4-6

A pinch of saffron
2 carrots
1 onion
2 celery sticks
2 leeks
5 tablespoons olive oil
Sea salt
750g firm white fish fillets, such
  as monkfish
200g shellfish (prawns in their
  shells, mussels, etc)
500g new waxy potatoes
1 teaspoon ground coriander
½ teaspoon ground cumin
1 litre fish stock
2 bay leaves
1 teaspoon black peppercorns
2 lemons
½ bunch of flat-leaf parsley or
  coriander, or a combination
1 green chilli

Place the saffron in a small bowl and pour over 50ml of just-boiled water and set aside. Peel and finely chop the carrots and onion. Trim and finely slice the celery and leeks, making sure to give the leeks a good rinse to get rid of any dirt. Place a large flameproof casserole or saucepan on a medium-low heat and add the olive oil. Add all the chopped vegetables to the pan, season generously with sea salt and sauté for 30 minutes, stirring occasionally, until everything is softened and sticky.

Meanwhile, cut the fish into 3cm chunks. Clean the shellfish; I like to butterfly the prawns in their shells. Cut the potatoes into 2.5cm chunks. When the vegetables are ready, stir in the ground coriander and ground cumin. Fry for a couple of minutes then add the fish stock, bay leaves, peppercorns and cut potatoes to the pan. Squeeze in the juice of one lemon. Bring to the boil, cook for 15 minutes, then add the fish. Cook for a further 7 minutes and then check a piece of fish; it may need another minute or three. While it's cooking, finely chop the herbs. Halve, deseed and finely slice the chilli. Stir the herbs through the soup, taste and season with the juice from the remaining lemon and serve with the sliced green chilli on top.

Tserepa: *roast chicken, potatoes and peppers*

Originally from Ithaca, this dish that's traditionally cooked in a clay pot (a *tserepa*) over charcoal can be found all around the Ionian islands. It's one of those simple meals that you can't stop thinking about. The marinated meat, slowly cooked, is tender; the potatoes absorb the chicken fat and juices; and there's sweetness from the tomatoes and peppers. It's the epitome of effortless cooking.

SERVES 4

4 chicken legs, thigh and leg
  pieces (about 1kg in total)
Sea salt and freshly ground
  black pepper
6 garlic cloves
3 tablespoons olive oil, plus a little
  extra for frying
2 large or 3 small green peppers
3 ripe tomatoes
600g waxy potatoes
A handful of stoned black olives
2 tablespoons tomato purée
250ml white wine
1 lemon
1 tablespoon oregano

Place the chicken in a bowl or plastic bag and season generously with salt and pepper. Crush in the garlic and add the olive oil. Massage into the chicken and leave to marinate for as long as possible, overnight if you have time. If you have no time, don't worry.

Preheat your oven to 170°C/150°C fan/gas mark 3½. Place a large flameproof casserole on a medium heat, drizzle in a little olive oil and fry the chicken, skin-side down, for about 10 minutes, until golden. Meanwhile, remove the tops and seeds of the green peppers and slice the flesh into 1cm-thick rounds. Slice the tomatoes to the same thickness. Halve the potatoes if they're small, or cut larger ones into four slices. Roughly chop the olives.

When the chicken is browned, remove and leave to one side. Stir the tomato purée into the pan and fry for a minute or two. Add the wine and bring to the boil. Stir in the potatoes, peppers, tomato slices and olives. Squeeze in the juice of the lemon and sprinkle in the oregano. Season with salt and pepper and mix together well. Nestle the chicken in, skin-side up, so it's slightly submerged. There should be enough liquid in the pan that it comes up the side of the vegetables by only just less than 1cm. If it's below that level, add a splash of boiling water. Cover with the lid and roast in the oven for 1 hour and 15 minutes, until everything is tender and cooked through. After 1 hour, remove the lid and increase the oven temperature to 200°C/180°C fan/gas mark 6 for the last 15 minutes, to get a little colour.

Roast chicken with tomatoey bulgur wheat

This is a gorgeous roast chicken – the way the spiced marinade flavours the bird and then the bulgur wheat is heaven. In my family, we'd never eat bulgur without a dollop of yoghurt on the side. I don't even know why anymore, but I urge you to try it here: its creamy tang beautifully complements the sweet-acidic tomatoes. I like to serve this one-pot wonder with the dilly leeks and peas (see page 210).

SERVES 4–6

1.7kg whole chicken
2 teaspoons dried oregano
½ teaspoon ground cinnamon
½ teaspoon sweet smoked paprika
Sea salt and freshly ground
 black pepper
Olive oil
400g ripe tomatoes
4 garlic cloves
1 tablespoon tomato purée
750ml chicken stock
150g sun-dried tomatoes
250g bulgur wheat
250g Greek yoghurt (dairy-free,
 if needed), optional

Preheat your oven to 200°C/180°C fan/gas mark 6. Place the chicken in a flameproof casserole and sprinkle with the oregano, cinnamon and paprika. Season generously with salt and pepper and drizzle with olive oil. Rub all the flavours into the chicken. Roughly chop the tomatoes and place in a blender. Peel and add the garlic, the tomato purée and 250ml of the chicken stock. Blitz until smooth and then pour around the chicken, spooning a little over the top. Roughly chop the sun-dried tomatoes and add them to the pan. Place the casserole on the hob and bring everything to the boil. Transfer the pan to the oven and roast for 1 hour.

When the hour is almost up, place the remaining stock in a saucepan and bring to the boil. Take the casserole out of the oven and carefully remove the chicken to a plate. Stir the bulgur wheat into the casserole with the hot stock, then nestle the chicken back in the casserole with the stock and bulgur. Return to the oven for a further 15 minutes, until the bulgur is cooked, then remove from the oven. Leave it to rest 10 minutes before carving the bird, spooning out the bulgur and serving with a generous dollop of Greek yoghurt, if you like.

Pulled chicken gyro with all the trimmings

DF + GF

The marinade in this recipe is an absolute favourite of mine because it is so versatile. I use it for pork or lamb, occasionally firm white fish, but most often with chicken. It's great to marinate drumsticks in for a barbecue. You could use it with chicken thigh fillets, then double skewer them, piled on top of each other, to create a DIY gyro. *Gyro* means 'to turn around' — revolve, or gyrate — so refers to the way meat is cooked on a vertical spit with a motor. This recipe doesn't involve any turning — it's not realistic with most people's home set-ups — so I use 'gyro' here to refer to the way the meat is shredded, wrapped and the accompaniments it's eaten with. If you have a spit, go ahead and get turning.

SERVES 6

3 garlic cloves
250g Greek yoghurt (dairy-free, if needed)
3 lemons
3 tablespoons olive oil, plus extra for roasting
1½ teaspoons sweet smoked paprika, plus extra to serve
1 tablespoon ground coriander
1 teaspoon ground cinnamon
1 tablespoon dried oregano
Sea salt and freshly ground black pepper
1 chicken (about 1.6kg), spatchcocked (page 270)

To serve

6 fluffy flatbreads (gluten-free, if needed) — shop-bought or make your own (page 34)
Sliced tomatoes, finely sliced red onion and pickled chillies; if you want to be authentic, sneak in some chips (page 146)
Tzatziki, plain Greek yoghurt or mustard sauce (page 146)

Peel and finely grate the garlic into a large container or plastic bag with the Greek yoghurt, the juice of one lemon, the olive oil, the paprika, coriander, cinnamon and most of the oregano. Add a generous pinch of salt and pepper and mix together. Place the spatchcocked chicken in the marinade, really rubbing it into all the nooks and crannies. Cover and place in the fridge for at least 5 hours, ideally overnight.

Remove the chicken from the fridge 20 minutes before you are ready to cook to let it come up to room temperature. Preheat your oven to 210°C/190°C fan/gas mark 6½. Wipe off the excess marinade from the chicken before placing it in a roasting tray. Carefully pour a little boiling water into the bottom of the tray, about 75ml. Drizzle the chicken with a little olive oil and place in the oven for 50-60 minutes, until the skin is deep golden-brown and the meat is tender and cooked through. Leave to one side to rest for 15 minutes, then use two forks to shred the meat from the carcass, letting the meat fall directly into the tray and all the sticky juices. (Alternatively, you can use gloves, or clean hands, and pull the meat apart.) Discard any flabby bits of skin or fat.

Heat the flatbreads just before serving. I like to wave them over the direct flame of the hob for a few seconds. You could also wrap them in foil and warm them in the residual heat of the oven. Pile the chicken on the warm flatbreads and top with all the extras and sauce you want, then sprinkle over the remaining oregano and extra paprika. Quarter the remaining lemons and serve the wedges for squeezing over.

Pork shoulder, beans and chard

DF + GF

Pork shoulder is my joint of choice for roasting. People think that Greeks love lamb, which is true, but Cypriots in particular really love pork. I appreciate how little attention a shoulder needs; give it enough time in a low oven and it rewards your negligence. To make this an even less demanding meal, the beans and greens cook in the pan with it. You could serve this dish with a small salad, or some bread or potatoes, but it's not really necessary.

SERVES 6-8

1 lemon, plus extra to serve
 (optional)
6 garlic cloves
½ bunch of rosemary
Sea salt and freshly ground
 black pepper
5 tablespoons olive oil, plus
 a little extra
2kg rolled pork shoulder, skin-on
 and scored
3 onions
4 celery sticks
175ml white wine
2 × 400g tins of cannellini or
 butter beans
300ml chicken stock
2 bay leaves
300g chard

Finely grate the lemon into a mini food processor (alternatively, you could do this with a pestle and mortar). Add the peeled garlic cloves and pick in the rosemary leaves. Blitz together, then squeeze in the lemon juice, season well and add two tablespoons of olive oil. Pulse until you have a thick paste. Rub half of the paste over the pork and leave to one side for half an hour. If you have time, you can marinate this for longer and leave covered in the fridge for several hours or even overnight.

Preheat your oven to 240°C/220°C fan/gas mark 9. Peel the onions and cut them into wedges. Trim the celery and cut into 3cm pieces. Place a large flameproof casserole on the hob, and drizzle in three tablespoons of olive oil. Add the onions, celery and remaining garlic paste. Fry for 5 minutes, then add the white wine and bring to the boil. Pour in both tins of the beans with their juice, then add the chicken stock and bay leaves and bring everything to the boil. Nestle in the pork joint, so it sits on top of the beans. Rub the skin of the pork with a little olive oil and place the casserole in the oven. Cook for 30 minutes, so the skin starts to crisp.

While the pork is in the oven, roughly slice the chard. After 30 minutes, remove the casserole from the oven. Stir the chard through the beans, cover the casserole with a lid and return to the oven. Reduce the heat to 160°C/140°C fan/gas mark 3. Cook the pork for 3-3½ hours, or until the meat is tender. To finish, remove the lid and turn the heat back up to 240°C/220°C fan/gas mark 9 for a final 20 minutes, to help the skin crisp up. Remove from the oven, rest the meat for 15 minutes, then serve as is or with a little extra lemon juice over the top.

Triple-fennel pork belly

This recipe has a fancy restaurant-style name, but it's a simple idea that comes from my love of pairing fennel and pork, and Greek people's love of fennel in all forms. The bulb is used in cooking, the leaf herb is used in pies and salads, and the seeds are used to make tea. Historically it was believed that fennel tea gave courage to warriors before battle, and it was said that Prometheus used a stalk of fennel to carry fire from Mount Olympus to Earth. Here, the fennel seeds flavour the meat, the bulb cooks down to make a sweet base, and the third use of fennel is in a slaw to bring a much-needed freshness to counter quite a rich joint of meat. This is brilliant with the sliced potatoes (page 197). If you have any leftover meat and base, the next day roughly chop it and toss it through pasta. So good.

SERVES 6

1.8kg pork belly, on the bone,
 skin scored
1 ½ tablespoons fennel seeds
1 teaspoon coriander seeds
Sea salt and freshly ground
 black pepper
600ml chicken stock
4 onions
3 fennel bulbs
1 whole garlic bulb
100g stoned green olives
175ml white wine
1 tablespoon honey
1 teaspoon Dijon mustard
3 tablespoons white wine vinegar
Extra virgin olive oil
1 large bunch of coriander

Pat the skin of the pork belly dry. Crush the fennel and coriander seeds and rub into the pork skin along with two teaspoons of sea salt, pushing it into all the scoring. Leave to one side for 30 minutes.

Preheat your oven to the highest temperature it will go to, ideally about 250°C/230°C fan/maximum gas mark. Heat the stock in a pan. Peel, halve and slice three of the onions. Trim and slice two of the fennel bulbs into thin wedges. Cut the garlic bulb in half horizontally. Place the veg in a large roasting tray with the olives and pour in the wine and hot stock. Pop the pork on top and place in the oven. Roast for 25 minutes, till the skin starts to crackle, then turn the heat down to 140°C/120°C fan/gas mark 1 to cook low and slow for 4½–5 hours. You want the meat so tender that it falls apart when prodded. When it's done, turn the heat back up to the highest setting and cook for a further 30 minutes. This will re-crisp the crackling and reduce the base liquid. (If the base is quite reduced, you can also get crackling by popping it under a hot grill for less time, but keep an eye on it and don't have the pork too close to the grill — it burns so easily.) When the pork is crackled, set aside and leave to rest for 15 minutes.

While the pork rests, make the slaw. Peel and finely slice the remaining onion, on a mandoline or as finely as you can by hand. Trim and do the same with the remaining fennel bulb. In a mixing bowl, whisk the honey with the Dijon mustard and vinegar and season well with salt and pepper. Whisk in a couple of tablespoons of extra virgin olive oil. Finely chop the coriander stalks and chop the leaves. Toss all the coriander in the dressing bowl with the onion and fennel and really mix well. Serve the salad with the pork belly and spoonfuls of the fennelly base.

Youvetsi: *my favourite meat and orzo stew*

This all-in-one stew is home for many Greeks, pure nostalgia and comfort. It is yiayia's handmade floral apron, that bowl you ate cereal from at your nan's house, the hug you need after your day has been a bit pants, a big bowl of food that says: 'I love you. Eat.' It's one of those dishes that doesn't look like much but you quickly realise is the most delicious thing you've had in ages. If I had to sum up Greeks and Cypriots as people, it would be with a dish like this.

SERVES 6

2kg beef short rib (bone-in), or
  1.2kg boneless lamb or pork
  shoulder
800ml beef stock
Sea salt and freshly ground
  black pepper
Olive oil
2 onions
3 garlic cloves
2 carrots
2 celery sticks
½ bunch of thyme
1 heaped tablespoon tomato purée
175ml red wine
400ml passata
1 teaspoon caster sugar
1 bay leaf
300g orzo (gluten-free, if needed)
100g halloumi (optional)

Preheat the oven to 160°C/140°C fan/gas mark 3 . To take your short rib off the bone, use the tip of a sharp knife and simply follow the meat along the bone. It's easiest to do this if you place the meat side flat on a board, then just cut the bone away, gradually lifting off the bone as you go. Trim down the sides of each rib. Place the rib bones, and any large bits of fat you've trimmed away, in a saucepan and simmer along with the stock. Slice the rib meat into pieces about 5cm square. If using lamb or pork, cut it into similar-sized pieces.

Season the meat well. Place a large flameproof casserole or wide ovenproof pan on a medium heat and drizzle in a good glug of olive oil. Fry the meat, in batches if needed, until browned all over — about 2-3 minutes on each side. Remove the meat to a plate and set aside. Meanwhile, peel and finely chop the onions, garlic, carrots and trim and finely chop the celery. If you like, you can strip the leaves off the thyme sprigs, but I sometimes just chuck in the branches. Add all the chopped vegetables to the pan with the thyme and fry for 10 minutes, reducing the heat a little. Add the tomato purée and fry, stirring, for 2 minutes, then add the wine, scraping any sticky bits off the bottom of the pan. Reduce the wine by half, then add the passata and 150ml of the stock. (Take the remaining stock off the heat.) Stir in the caster sugar and bay leaf and return the meat back to the pan. Bring to the boil then cover. Place in the oven for 2½ hours.

Just before you remove the casserole from the oven, heat the remaining 650ml beef stock till it boils. Remove the pan from the oven and carefully add in the stock and stir in the orzo. Cover again and bake for a further 30 minutes. The orzo should be perfectly cooked, the liquid thickened and the meat tender. Grate over the halloumi, if using, just before serving.

Pastitsada: *spiced beef with pasta*

Originally from Corfu, pastitsada is inspired by the slow-cooked meat dishes of northern Italy. It is a 'throw it all together in 20 minutes' dish that is rich and intense and laced with a warming blend of spices such as cinnamon, cloves, allspice and black pepper. In Corfu you can buy the blend already made, called *spetseriko* (it was originally sold in pharmacies as it was used medicinally but is now found in grocers). I've picked out key flavours, but tweak to your liking, adding more cinnamon or even cumin, if you like.

The long cooking time is made more bearable by the otherwise lack of involvement this sauce requires. You can leave it to tick away unattended until needed. If I am using the oven to make something else, I cook it in there on a low heat, as I think it intensifies the sauce a little, but it's perfectly happy on the hob. You could make the beef element ahead of time (we know all slow braises taste better the next day) and finish with pasta and cheese as needed.

SERVES 6

1kg boneless beef shin
Sea salt and freshly ground
 black pepper
2 tablespoons olive oil
2 onions
2 carrots
2 celery sticks
2 garlic cloves
½ teaspoon sweet smoked paprika
½ teaspoon ground allspice
½ ground mixed spice
1 tablespoon tomato purée
1 x 400g tin of plum tomatoes
1 bay leaf
600ml beef stock
500g striftaria or trofie
 (gluten-free, if needed)
75g kefalotyri or pecorino

Cut the beef into even chunks, about 3cm, and season well. Place a large flameproof casserole on a high heat and drizzle in the olive oil. Fry the beef (in batches, if needed) for about 10 minutes, turning occasionally, until browned all over, then transfer to a plate.

While the beef is frying, prepare the vegetables. Peel and chop the onions and carrots, but not too small. Trim and slice the celery. Peel and finely chop the garlic. Once the beef is browned, reduce the heat to medium-low and add all the chopped veg to the casserole. Fry for 10 minutes, then stir in the paprika, ground allspice, mixed spice and tomato purée and fry for a minute. Add the beef back in, then stir in the tinned tomatoes, bay leaf and stock and bring to the boil. Break the tomatoes up with a wooden spoon. Cover, reduce the heat to low and simmer for 3-3½ hours, or until the beef is very tender (give it an occasional stir). Remove the lid for the last 30 minutes to thicken the sauce. Taste and adjust the seasoning.

When the beef is cooked, bring a big saucepan of salted water to the boil and cook the pasta according to the packet instructions until al dente. Drain the pasta, reserving a mug of the water, and toss the pasta through the beef. Keep stirring, and add the pasta water until the sauce is amalgamated and silky. To finish, grate over the kefalotyri and add a good sprinkle of freshly ground black pepper.

Kreatopites: *little meat pies*

Greeks love a pita (pie) and will make almost anything into one. Kreatopites (meat pies) take many guises across the country. I am particularly fond of a Kefalonian kreatopita, which involves slowly cooking three kinds of meat with rice and vegetables before stuffing it into homemade filo. It's delicious and rich, but also labour intensive — not the kind of thing to make often at home. This recipe is my favourite way to make a meat pie. The mince filling is deeply savoury and it's easy to make these individual pies in little rose shapes. If you want to make a bit of a showstopper, keep adding each length to build one large coil, cook it for a little longer and serve in slices.

SERVES 4

1 onion
2 garlic cloves
2 leeks
½ bunch of flat-leaf parsley
1 teaspoon cumin seeds
Olive oil
100g butter
500g mince (beef and lamb are
  traditional, but some people use
  them blended with pork)
Sea salt and freshly ground
  pepper
1 teaspoon ground cinnamon
1 teaspoon ground coriander
2 tablespoons tomato purée
1 teaspoon caster sugar
400ml beef stock
300g filo

Peel and finely chop the onion and garlic. Trim and finely slice the leeks and then wash well in a colander to remove any grit. Finely chop the flat-leaf parsley, stalks and all. Roughly crush the cumin seeds. Place a large frying pan on a medium-high heat and add a drizzle of olive oil and 25g of the butter. Add the mince, season generously and fry for 5–8 minutes, until the meat is starting to brown, breaking it up with a wooden spoon as you go. When it's starting to colour, reduce the heat and add the chopped vegetables. Sauté for 5 minutes, then add the cinnamon, coriander and most of the crushed cumin seeds. Fry for a few more minutes, then stir in the tomato purée, sugar and chopped parsley. Fry for a minute, stirring everything well, then add the stock and bring to the boil. Reduce the heat a little and leave it to gently simmer for 15–20 minutes, until the mince has a little moisture but most of the liquid has evaporated. Turn off the heat and leave to cool completely.

When you're ready to roll, preheat the oven to 210°C/190°C/gas mark 6½. Melt the remaining butter and brush a little over a large flat baking sheet or roasting tin. Lay a sheet of filo out, the longer side facing you. Brush the filo with a little butter and top with a second sheet. Spoon a long line of the mince mixture along the bottom. Working from the bottom, roll it up, then shape it into a coil. Place on the baking sheet. Repeat with the rest of the ingredients so you have four pies. Brush the pies all over with the remaining butter and sprinkle with a good pinch of sea salt and the remaining cumin seeds. Bake for about 30 minutes, until deep golden all over, then leave to cool for at least 10 minutes before eating.

Lamb shank fricassee with preserved lemon

Using a whisked egg and lemon mixture is a popular way to thicken sauces all over Greece and Cyprus. If you haven't ever tried this, it might seem like a difficult idea to get on board with, but trust me. The mixture gives a dish a satiny feel as the eggs gently cook and enrich the sauce, and the lemon brings a welcome fresh tang. It's the perfect way to finish this tender lamb braise that looks and tastes like spring in a pan.

SERVES 4

4 lamb shanks, 400g each
Sea salt and freshly ground
 black pepper
Olive oil
1 bunch of spring onions
4 garlic cloves
2 preserved lemons
1 bunch of flat-leaf parsley
1.25 litres chicken stock
A pinch of saffron (optional)
2 little gem lettuces
2 heads of endive or green chicory
½ bunch of dill
4 large eggs
2 lemons

DF + GF

Season the lamb shanks well with salt and pepper. Place a good drizzle of olive oil in a large casserole or pan on a medium heat. Fry the lamb shanks for about 10 minutes, turning, until they are browned all over. Meanwhile, trim and cut the spring onions in 1-2cm slices, then peel and finely slice the garlic. Cut the preserved lemons in half, scoop out and discard the flesh and pips, and finely slice the skin. Finely chop the parsley, stalks and all. When the lamb is ready, push it to one side in the pan and add the spring onions, garlic and the preserved lemon skin. Sauté for 5 minutes. Stir in the parsley, then pour in the stock. Add the pinch of saffron (if using) and bring everything to the boil. Cover with a lid, reduce the heat and simmer for 2½ hours, or until the lamb is tender. Depending on the size of your pan, you may need to turn the lamb over a few times if the shanks aren't totally submerged in the stock.

When the lamb is almost ready, trim, wash and slice the little gem and endive. Pick and chop the dill fronds. Add the chopped salad and most of the chopped dill to the pan and cook for a further 10 minutes.

Crack the eggs into a large mixing bowl, season well and squeeze in the juice of the lemons. Whisk until smooth and foamy. Working quickly, ladle some hot stock from the lamb into the egg mixture — keep whisking to prevent it scrambling. Do this with a few ladles of hot stock until you have a smooth mixture. Pour the egg mixture into the casserole, stirring into the stock until combined, then warm through for only a minute or two. You want the base to become creamy and rich, but not bubble and scramble. Remove from the heat and leave uncovered, so the fricassee thickens as it cools. Serve with the remaining dill sprinkled over the top.

Slow-roasted 30 garlic lamb shoulder

Everyone needs a good Sunday roast in their repertoire and this is a simple recipe to learn by heart. Make it yours however you like: add more or less garlic; consider different woody herbs — a bit of bay or thyme; try a different vinegar... Just keep the technique and overall flavour balance the same and it will quickly become a welcome, classic addition to your table.

SERVES 6

30 garlic cloves
½ bunch of rosemary
2kg lamb shoulder, bone-in
4 tablespoons red wine vinegar
3 tablespoons honey
2 tablespoons olive oil
Sea salt and freshly ground
 black pepper
250ml beef or chicken stock
4 red onions

If you can, marinate the lamb at least a couple of hours ahead of cooking. Peel the garlic cloves, and pick half of the rosemary sprigs. Make about 20 incisions in the lamb and poke in some small garlic cloves (halving any larger ones) and rosemary sprigs. In a non-reactive dish big enough to hold the lamb, mix together the red wine vinegar, two tablespoons of honey and the olive oil and season generously. Whisk together and add the lamb shoulder, rubbing the marinade all over. Place the remaining garlic cloves in the dish. Cover and leave in the fridge until needed.

When you are ready to cook the lamb, preheat your oven to its highest setting and heat the stock in a small pan. Peel the onions and cut them into wedges 2cm thick. Line a roasting tray that's just big enough to hold the lamb with greaseproof paper. Add the onion wedges, place the lamb on top and pour in all the extra marinade. Pour in the hot stock. Drizzle with the remaining honey and cover the tray tightly with foil. Place in the oven and immediately reduce the heat to 150°C/130°C fan/gas mark 2. Cook slowly for 4 hours, then check the lamb. You want it to be perfectly tender, so have a check, and if it's not there yet, pop it back in the oven for another hour.

When the lamb is tender, take it out of the oven and remove the foil. Baste the lamb with the juices and turn the oven temperature up to 220°C/200°C fan/gas mark 7. Return to the oven and roast for a final 30 minutes, so the meat and fat crisp up and get a nice colour. Remove the tray from the oven. Leave the lamb to rest for at least 15 minutes before shredding in the pan, tossing in all the juices. Alternatively, remove to a platter and spoon around all of the sweet onions and garlic.

The classic: watermelon, feta and cucumber
Sticky date and tahini aubergine
Crispy cauliflower and lentils with herby green olive dressing
Roasted lemon, oregano and feta potatoes
Patates antinahtes: pan-fried new potatoes with red wine
 and coriander
Mum's sliced potatoes
Cabbage, green bean and sesame salad
Roasted beets with caramelised nuts
Fried and pickled peppers
Charred green beans, asparagus and almonds
Honeymoon tomatoes, avocado and anchovies
Corn on the cob with thyme and burnt butter
Crispy rice, pomegranate and herb salad
Dilly leeks and peas
Simple pilafi
Roasted squash, kataifi and pomegranate salad

Salads, sides & vegetables

The classic: *watermelon, feta and cucumber*

I like to get creative with some recipes, embellish or make them my own in some way. Others are perfection already. This summertime salad is just that. It's Greece on a plate. No messing.

SERVES 4

½ red onion
2 tablespoons red wine vinegar
Sea salt and freshly ground
 black pepper
500g watermelon
½ cucumber
½ bunch of mint
4 tablespoons extra virgin olive oil
200g feta

Peel and finely slice the red onion. Place in a large mixing bowl with the red wine vinegar and a good pinch of salt, and toss together. Leave to one side for 10 minutes, to lightly pickle. Meanwhile, peel and chop the watermelon into 2cm pieces, discarding any black pips you find. Halve the cucumber lengthwise and scoop out and discard the seeds (or save for the recipe on page 256). Slice the cucumber into 5mm half-moons. Pick and finely shred the mint leaves. Add the watermelon, cucumber and mint to the red onion and toss everything together with the extra virgin olive oil. Season well and leave for 5 minutes to macerate. Crumble in the feta and serve straight away.

V + GF

Sticky date and tahini aubergine

VG + GF

If I could dog-ear the corner of this page for you, I would have done so already. It might be one of the best recipes in the book. It is everything I like in a salad: sweet, salty, spicy. If cooking aubergines has ever felt intimidating, this is the way to start — it's foolproof.

SERVES 4

3 aubergines
4 tablespoons olive oil
Sea salt and freshly ground
 black pepper
150g Greek yoghurt (plant-based,
 if needed)
1 garlic clove
1 lemon
½ bunch of mint
½ bunch of coriander
3 tablespoons tahini
3 tablespoons date syrup/
 molasses
1 tablespoon extra virgin olive oil
125g medjool dates
½ teaspoon ground coriander
¼ teaspoon ground cumin
½ teaspoon Aleppo pepper (or ¼
 teaspoon dried red chilli flakes),
 plus extra for sprinkling

Preheat your oven to 220°C/200°C fan/gas mark 7. Trim the aubergines and use a peeler to remove most of the skin in strips. Slice the peeled aubergines into 3cm-thick rounds and place in a large bowl. Drizzle with the olive oil and season generously with sea salt and black pepper and massage in. Lay the aubergine slices in a roasting tray (or two; you don't want the slices to overlap). Roast for 30 minutes.

Meanwhile, spoon the Greek yoghurt into a mixing bowl and finely grate in the garlic. Season generously, then squeeze in half the lemon juice. Pick the mint and coriander leaves; set half aside for later, and finely chop the rest and stir into the yoghurt. In another bowl, whisk the tahini with three tablespoons of cold water, the remaining lemon juice, one tablespoon of date syrup and the extra virgin olive oil, and season really well. Remove the stones from the dates and roughly chop the flesh.

After the aubergine has had 30 minutes in the oven, remove and drizzle with the remaining date syrup. Sprinkle over the ground coriander, ground cumin and half the Aleppo pepper. Add the chopped dates to the tray, carefully toss everything together and return to the oven for a further 5-8 minutes, until sticky and caramelised. Spoon the yoghurt over a serving platter and top with the sticky aubergines and dates. Drizzle over the tahini dressing and scatter over the reserved herbs and extra Aleppo pepper just before serving.

Crispy cauliflower and lentils with herby green olive dressing

VG + GF

Salads like this are a real weeknight staple for me — flexible and nutritious. If I don't have cauliflower, I replace it with broccoli. If I want spice, I add chilli. Roasting the lentils gives them a wonderful crunchy, nutty texture. You could even use the whole tin if you don't want to store leftovers; you'll just need to increase the dressing a little. Serve it as a side, or as a meal in its own right, perhaps with some grilled halloumi. It also makes a great lunchbox the next day.

SERVES 4 AS A SIDE

1 cauliflower (about 900g)
½ × 400g tin of lentils, drained
4 tablespoons olive oil
Sea salt and freshly ground
 black pepper
100g stoned green olives
1 ½ tablespoons red wine vinegar
1 teaspoon honey (or maple syrup,
 to make it vegan)
½ bunch of flat-leaf parsley
A few sprigs of basil

Preheat your oven to 240°C/220°C fan/gas mark 9. Cut the cauliflower into even florets. Place them in a large roasting tray with the drained lentils. Toss with two tablespoons of olive oil. Season well and spread out evenly. Roast in the oven for 15-18 minutes, until golden, crisping up at the edges and just cooked through.

While the cauliflower is cooking, make the dressing. Roughly chop the olives and place in the bowl of a mini food processor. Add the red wine vinegar and honey. Chop the flat-leaf parsley and basil and add half to the bowl along with two tablespoons of olive oil. Blitz until finely chopped but not too smooth or like a paste — you want to keep a bit of texture. (You can do this by hand if you prefer; finely chop the olives and herbs, then stir in a bowl with the olive oil.) When the cauliflower is ready, toss through the dressing and adjust the seasoning. You can serve this hot or at room temperature, but just before you do, toss through the remaining herbs.

Roasted lemon, oregano and feta potatoes

You know when something is simple and obvious and so good that you kick yourself for not making it more often? These potatoes are just that. My yiayia Martha makes them as a massive tray and I can never stop picking at them — I think it's because she uses a bit more salt or lemon or seasoning than I do. Lesson learned.

SERVES 4

1kg waxy potatoes, Cyprus if possible
1 stock cube (chicken or vegetable)
100ml olive oil
2 teaspoons dried oregano
2 lemons
6 garlic cloves
Sea salt and freshly ground black pepper
100g feta

Preheat your oven to 200°C/180°C fan/gas mark 6. Peel the potatoes, then cut them into large wedges. Place in a roasting tray large enough to hold them all in a single layer. Dissolve the stock cube in a jug with 250ml of boiling water. Whisk in the olive oil and dried oregano, then squeeze in the juice from both the lemons. Crush or finely grate in the garlic and then season generously. Whisk again to combine, then pour over the potatoes, and turn a few times to distribute all the flavours. Shake out the potatoes so they're in one layer. Place the tray in the oven and roast for 1 hour, then carefully turn the potatoes over. The stock at this point should have cooked away. Cook for a further 25-30 minutes, until the potatoes are golden and crisp. Finish by crumbling over the feta, and serve.

V + GF

Patates antinahtes: *pan-fried new potatoes with red wine and coriander*

I've never seen this unusual recipe, or even a variation of it, outside of the Greek Cypriot community. It is unbelievably good. These spuds are often referred to as patates afelia, because the method and ingredients mirror those in afelia, a famous Cypriot pork dish. The potatoes don't taste winey or boozy at all, but are slightly caramelised, with the wine just adding a deeper flavour and slight sweetness. They are great hot but also amazing when they're at room temperature, and are ideal to snack on while you're having a drink.

SERVES 6

1kg new potatoes
500-700ml olive or vegetable oil
2 teaspoons coriander seeds
½ teaspoon cumin seeds
Sea salt
150ml red wine

The trick to patates antinahtes is cracking the potatoes. Do this one by one using a pestle and mortar, just hitting the potato enough to split it once, so it has only one crack — any more and they will disintegrate. Place the cracked potatoes in a large saucepan. Pour in enough oil to just cover the potatoes and pop the pan on a medium heat. Cook for about 10-15 minutes, until the potatoes are tender and golden. You don't want the oil to be spitting or vigorous, just ticking away. As soon as they are ready, carefully strain away most of the oil (use it for another recipe), leaving just enough to coat the potatoes.

Roughly crush the coriander seeds and cumin seeds, then stir through the potatoes with one teaspoon of sea salt and the red wine. Bring to the boil and then cover the pan. Cook for only 3-4 minutes, until the wine has been absorbed. Remove from the heat. Either serve straight away as a side or leave to cool and snack on, like I do.

VG + GF

Mum's sliced potatoes

One of our favourite dinners growing up was chicken Kyiv, Mum's sliced potatoes and boiled buttered veg — a meal I would happily eat today! Her hand-sliced potatoes would be layered at an angle in a round tin, perfectly seasoned, cooked until golden and crisp around the edges. I could pick away at that tin all evening. I now make them for my daughters, in an almost identical round metal tin, hoping to instil that nostalgic feeling.

SERVES 4

1 lemon
1kg potatoes — I like using Maris Piper for this
3 garlic cloves
5 tablespoons olive oil
Sea salt and freshly ground black pepper
A few sprigs of oregano or 1 heaped teaspoon dried oregano

Get yourself a bowl of cold water and squeeze in a little lemon juice. You can peel the potatoes if you have time or feel inclined, but Mum doesn't always — up to you. The key thing is to slice them as finely as you can. Less than 3mm if possible. My mum has amazing knife skills, but I find it easier to use the slicing attachment on my food processor (or a mandoline). Pop them in the acidulated water as you slice them.

When you're ready, preheat your oven to 200°C/180°C fan/gas mark 6. Peel and finely grate the garlic into a small bowl and add the olive oil. Squeeze in the remaining lemon juice, season with two teaspoons of salt and ½ teaspoon of pepper and pick in the oregano leaves, or add the dried oregano, if using that. Whisk everything together well.

Drain and dry the potatoes, then stack them up. Carefully place stacks on their edge in a round baking tin or cake tin (not one with a loose base) or in lines in a roasting tray, at an angle so they overlap. Pour the dressing evenly over the potatoes. Cover the tray with foil and pop in the oven for 30 minutes. Remove the foil and cook for a further 30-40 minutes, until the potatoes are tender and crisp around the edges. Serve from the tin.

Cabbage, green bean and sesame salad

You will find many versions of white cabbage salad in my books; it's another recipe my mum always made us. It has a place in all meal situations: on the side of hot meals, with grilled meats, as part of meze-style dining, or in a vegan feast. This iteration, with nutty toasted sesame, is my current favourite way of preparing it. I can't get enough.

SERVES 4

30g sesame seeds
150g green beans
½ white cabbage (about 400g)
1 onion
Sea salt and freshly ground
 black pepper
2 lemons
2 ripe tomatoes
1 bunch of coriander
3 tablespoons extra virgin olive oil

Toast the sesame seeds in a small dry saucepan on a medium heat until they turn golden. Remove from the pan and leave to one side to cool. Fill the pan with water and bring to the boil. Trim the green beans, cut into thirds and cook in the boiling water for 4 minutes. Drain and cool under cold running water. Leave to dry.

Halve the cabbage and remove and discard the core. Finely shred the cabbage and place in a large mixing bowl. Peel, halve and finely slice the onion. Add one teaspoon of sea salt to the bowl, and squeeze in the juice of the lemons. Scrunch everything together and leave to one side for 5 minutes. Meanwhile, cut the tomatoes into 1.5cm chunks, discarding any seeds that fall out. Chop the coriander, stalks and all. Add the tomatoes and coriander to the cabbage with the cooled, dry green beans and toss everything together with the extra virgin olive oil. Season with freshly ground black pepper and stir in the toasted sesame. Serve straight away (although it is still delicious after it has sat for a while).

VG + GF

Roasted beets with caramelised nuts

I love beetroot in all forms, and especially appreciate the vac-packed ones you get in supermarket and greengrocer fridges. They save you from having to peel and boil them yourself — and walking round with stained hands. They're incredibly versatile; you can eat them as they are, and they're great for roasting. Here, I've pan-fried them to get a sticky glaze, a great cheat that mimics an effect that could take hours in an oven for raw ones.

SERVES 4

500g cooked whole beetroot (not
 in vinegar)
A knob of unsalted butter (use
 plant-based, if needed)
Olive oil
½ teaspoon sweet smoked paprika
1 teaspoon honey (or maple syrup)
Sea salt and freshly ground
 black pepper
½ lemon
30g almonds
1 tablespoon sesame seeds
2 teaspoons caster sugar
1 teaspoon sumac
½ bunch of flat-leaf parsley
150g Greek yoghurt (plant-based,
 if needed)
½ garlic clove

Chop the beets into 2-3cm pieces. Add the butter to a medium-large heavy-based frying pan along with a drizzle of olive oil, the sweet smoked paprika and honey, and season well. Put the pan on a medium heat and leave to bubble and mix together. Stir in the beetroot and toss to coat in the glaze. Fry for 15 minutes, until sticky, stirring occasionally. When the beetroot is hot through with caramelised edges, squeeze in the lemon to deglaze and turn off the heat. Leave to one side to cool slightly.

Meanwhile, roughly chop the almonds. Place in a dry frying pan with the sesame seeds and toast on a medium heat for a few minutes. Stir in the caster sugar, then after a minute remove the pan from the heat and stir in the sumac. Roughly chop the parsley. Spoon the Greek yoghurt into a mixing bowl. Peel and finely grate in the garlic. Stir through the slightly cooled beetroot, so the yoghurt becomes garishly pink, and spoon out onto a serving plate. Top with the toasted nuts and seeds and the chopped parsley just before serving.

VG + GF

Fried and pickled peppers

Visit any Greek or Cypriot family for a feast and you're sure to find a plate of peeled onion quarters or a few whole spring onions, a cut-up lemon, peppers and probably a few green chillies (a Cypriot thing, for sure) to snack on with the meal. You can keep the peppers raw, but I love the kebab-shop vibes of adding vinegar and sugar. Make these ahead of time and leave to one side, at room temperature, until needed. A simple side for any hearty meal.

SERVES 4–6

300g small green or red peppers
 (about 8 of the little pointy ones)
Olive oil
3 tablespoons red wine vinegar
½ tablespoon caster sugar
Sea salt and freshly ground
 black pepper

Halve the peppers through the stalks and remove the seeds. Drizzle a few tablespoons of olive oil into a large frying pan and lay the peppers out in one layer. Place the pan on a medium-high heat and fry them for 3 minutes on each side. Sprinkle over the red wine vinegar and caster sugar, and season generously. Fry for a couple more minutes on each side, until glistening and softened. Remove from the pan and transfer to a serving plate. Serve at room temperature, alongside any meal.

(Photo on page 201)

VG + GF

Charred green beans, asparagus and almonds

I love cooking any greens this way, so they blister and char slightly in an almost dry pan. You can, of course, cook them on a griddle or barbecue with similar effect, but this way feels achievable for most kitchen set-ups. Depending on the season, you can use either or both vegetables. I love the fine, wild asparagus you get in Greece and Cyprus in early spring, then when the summer beans come in, I'll mix it up with whatever is available.

SERVES 4

150g fine green beans
150g young asparagus
 (thinner spears)
3 garlic cloves
20g flaked almonds
3 tablespoons olive oil
Sea salt and freshly ground
 black pepper
½ teaspoon Aleppo pepper (or
 ¼ teaspoon dried red chilli flakes)
1 tablespoon red wine vinegar

Trim the beans and make sure they are very dry. Snap and discard the woody ends from the asparagus. Peel and finely slice the garlic. Place a large frying pan on a medium-low heat and add the almonds to the pan. Toast until lightly golden, then transfer to a plate and set aside. Pour the olive oil into the pan and turn the heat up a little. When it is hot, add the beans and asparagus. Fry for a couple of minutes, then cover with a lid. Cook for 4 minutes, uncover, turn the vegetables over and cook for a further 2-3 minutes, until charred all over. Season everything generously, then add the Aleppo pepper and sliced garlic. Fry for a further minute until the garlic is golden, then stir in the vinegar and remove from the heat. Stir in the toasted almonds and serve.

(Photo on page 201)

VG + GF

Honeymoon tomatoes, avocado and anchovies

The honeymoon in this title doesn't refer to my own (happily spent backpacking around Indonesia), but the many spent in Santorini. When I first visited, I quickly understood why it was (and is) such a romantic and popular honeymoon destination. It's a breathtakingly beautiful island, brimming with loved-up couples sharing lobster pasta while looking out over the dramatic caldera at sunset. Tomatoes are in abundance in Santorini, and salads like this are standard fare. So, while this isn't a flashback to my own honeymoon, it reminds me of romance and sunny Santorini days.

SERVES 4

600g tomatoes
Sea salt and freshly ground
 black pepper
1 garlic clove
1 red onion
2 tablespoons red wine vinegar
½ teaspoon caster sugar
4 tablespoons extra virgin olive oil
½ bunch of Greek (or regular) basil
2 ripe avocados
8 anchovy fillets, in oil

Start by salting the tomatoes. Wipe and chop them into small wedges or chunks. Toss with ½ teaspoon of sea salt and place in a colander in the sink. Leave to drain while you get the dressing ready, stirring every few minutes to encourage excess moisture to be drawn out.

Peel and finely grate the garlic into a small bowl. Peel and finely slice the red onion. Add it to the garlic and stir in the red wine vinegar and caster sugar and season with sea salt and freshly ground black pepper. Mix together and set aside for 5 minutes. Whisk in the extra virgin olive oil. Pick the basil leaves and tear any larger ones.

When you are ready, halve and stone the avocados, then peel and cut into 1cm slices. Pat the tomatoes dry with kitchen paper and place in a large serving or mixing bowl with the dressing and torn basil. Add the avocado slices, tear in the anchovies, gently toss everything together and serve.

DF + GF

Corn on the cob with thyme and burnt butter

I have such strong memories from childhood of the corn sellers that would line the beachfronts in Cyprus. Little metal carts, a single hanging light bulb to illuminate the pans of corn grilling on bars. You'll occasionally still find them, in Greece as well as Cyprus, but they've been mostly taken over by flashier food trucks and trendy stalls. I love the thought of people out for the evening, perhaps having a stroll and thinking: 'You know what I really want? Corn on the cob.' But you really do. Even if I wasn't hungry, I'd always get one. This corn dressed in a simple buttery mix is my homage to the corn sellers. Eating it on the cob will always make me feel like a little girl.

SERVES 4

4 corn on the cob, ready-stripped
  and trimmed
60g unsalted butter
3 garlic cloves
5 sprigs of thyme
¼ teaspoon sweet smoked paprika
1 tablespoon honey
Sea salt and freshly ground
  black pepper

Bring a large saucepan of water to the boil then cook the corn cobs for 5-8 minutes, until tender (how long will depend on the size of your cobs). Meanwhile, place the butter in a small saucepan on a medium-low heat. Leave it to melt, then peel and finely grate in the garlic. Pick in the thyme leaves. Add the sweet smoked paprika and cook, swirling the pan, until the garlic and butter turn deep golden and smell toasted and delicious. Remove from the heat and stir in the honey and season generously. When the corn is cooked, drain and leave to steam-dry for a minute before generously basting with the sweet, herby butter.

V + GF

Crispy rice, pomegranate and herb salad

A conversation about how much I hate rice salads led me on the path to write a better recipe. Too often they feel like a dustbin for leftover, mediocre jarred antipasti, and the dressings are usually a bit stale and oily. There must be one rice salad I've eaten and enjoyed, I thought. Then I remembered nam khao, the famous Lao crispy rice salad. The method of frying the cooked rice until crisp then using it as a vehicle for a salty and sour dressing is brilliant, so I applied this principle to Greek flavours. The result is a rice salad I can definitely get on board with.

SERVES 4 AS A SIDE

160g long grain rice
Sea salt and freshly ground
 black pepper
2 garlic cloves
3 tablespoons olive oil
2 tablespoons pomegranate
 molasses
½ pomegranate
1 bunch of spring onions
1 bunch of dill
½ bunch of mint
1 teaspoon Aleppo pepper (or
 ½ teaspoon dried red chilli flakes)
1 tablespoon honey (or maple
 syrup, to make it vegan)

Wash the rice thoroughly in a sieve until the water runs clear. If you have time, soak it in cold water for 20 minutes. Bring a saucepan of salted water to the boil then cook the rice for 8 minutes, so there is still a little bite. Drain in a sieve, and rinse with cold water to cool quickly. Finely grate or crush the garlic into a mixing bowl. Whisk in two tablespoons of olive oil and one tablespoon of pomegranate molasses. When the rice is drained and cold, toss through the dressing. Put a large frying pan on a medium heat and spoon in the rice mixture. Really press it into the pan, spreading it out evenly. Fry for about 10 minutes, turning sections of the rice over just once or twice so it really gets a chance to caramelise.

Meanwhile, pick the pomegranate seeds and discard the pith. Trim and finely slice the spring onions. Pick and finely chop the dill fronds and mint leaves. Place them all in a large serving bowl with the Aleppo pepper and leave to one side.

Once the rice has had 10 minutes, drizzle with the honey and the final tablespoon of pomegranate molasses. Mix together then press it out into an even layer again and fry for a further 5 minutes to really crisp it well, turning the heat up a little if needed. Turn the heat off and leave the rice to cool in the pan. When it is cool, toss through the pomegranate and herb mixture with the final tablespoon of olive oil. Mix together well, adjust the seasoning to taste and serve.

VG + GF

Dilly leeks and peas

This is such a classic Greek way of cooking peas, braised in a tomatoey sauce. It's a take on pizeli yiahni, a main meal that consists of peas cooked with other vegetables such as carrots and potatoes, and is one of my favourites. This is more of a side dish, and I've suggested frozen peas for versatility. By all means, use fresh if they're in season. There's nothing more calming than sitting and podding a colander piled with pea pods.

SERVES 4

2 leeks
30g unsalted butter (plant-based, if needed)
Olive oil
1 tablespoon tomato purée
100ml white wine
250g frozen peas
Sea salt and freshly ground black pepper
½ bunch of dill
½ lemon

Trim and slice the leeks — I slice the white part into 1cm rings and the green part thinner. Give them a good wash in a colander to get rid of any dirt. Place a large saucepan or flameproof casserole on a medium heat and add the butter and enough olive oil to cover the base. Add the washed leeks and sauté for about 10 minutes, until they start to soften. Stir in the tomato purée. Add the white wine, bring to the boil and reduce by half. Add the peas and 200ml of water. Bring everything back to the boil, season generously and then reduce to a simmer. Cover and cook for about 15-20 minutes, or until everything is tender, creamy almost, and the liquid has reduced down. Finely chop the dill and stir in at the end with the lemon juice. Serve hot, cold or at room temperature.

(Photo on page 167)

VG + GF

Simple pilafi

One of the most popular side dishes in Greece and Cyprus is pourgouri pilafi, a simple side dish made from bulgur wheat. It's a great base or vehicle for almost any braise, slow-roast or meal with lots of sauce. This is my version. (Add chopped peeled tomatoes to it and it becomes one of my mum's favourite simple meals. She'll often sit down to a bowl of it with a huge dollop of the tangiest Greek yoghurt and a squeeze of lemon.)

SERVES 4

2 onions
Olive oil
Sea salt and freshly ground
 black pepper
150g vermicelli
800ml stock (vegetable or
 chicken)
1 cinnamon stick
200g bulgur wheat

Peel and finely slice the onions. Place a large saucepan on a medium-low heat and add a few tablespoons of olive oil and the sliced onions. Season them well and fry for 5 minutes. Break in the vermicelli and turn up the heat. Let the pasta brown for a few minutes, then add the stock to the pan. Add the cinnamon stick and bring to the boil. Stir in the bulgur wheat, season again and as soon as it's bubbling, cover with a lid and reduce the heat. Cook for 8 minutes then remove from the heat. Remove the lid, cover with a tea towel, then place the lid on top again (make sure this isn't near any open flames) — the tea towel will absorb excess moisture to help make the pilafi fluffy. Leave to rest for 5 minutes, then use a fork to fluff it up. I think this is perfect alongside most meals.

VG

Roasted squash, kataifi and pomegranate salad

Roasted squash is easily one of my favourite vegetables to include in a salad, as it's such a great friend to so many flavours and textures, and is hearty enough to feel filling. But a good hearty salad for me is all about balance. If I'm roasting the squash and it caramelises and becomes sweet, then I want crunch in there, I want some sourness and it'll need a fresh element to lift it. For the crunch I usually rely on croutons, nuts and seeds, but then I started thinking: why can't kataifi or filo be the crunch; why can't pastry be a crouton? It's a first for me and I can tell you that I am very much here for it. I've tried both kataifi and filo in this salad and they both work very well. Torn-up filo becomes sticky and caramelises, but I particularly love the crisp texture that comes with kataifi, which then absorbs the dressing. It makes for a very striking salad indeed.

SERVES 4-6

700g butternut squash
Olive oil
Sea salt and freshly ground
 black pepper
½ teaspoon cumin seeds
1 teaspoon coriander seeds
1 teaspoon ground cinnamon
30g unsalted butter
75g kataifi (or filo) pastry
2 ½ tablespoons pomegranate
 molasses
30g pumpkin seeds
½ pomegranate
200g feta
40g wild rocket
1 tablespoon red wine vinegar

Preheat your oven to 200°C/180°C fan/gas mark 6. Peel the squash and cut it into 3cm chunks. Place in a large roasting tray, drizzle with olive oil and season well. Lightly crush the cumin and coriander seeds. Sprinkle them over the squash with the ground cinnamon and toss it all together. Roast for 15 minutes.

Meanwhile, melt the butter, and drizzle over the kataifi or filo pastry. When the squash has had 15 minutes, nestle the pastry in the tray: strew the kataifi in loose bundles or scrunch up the filo into little roses — don't worry about being precise here. Return the tray to the oven for a further 15 minutes, then drizzle everything with the pomegranate molasses and pumpkin seeds. Give it a final 20-25 minutes in the oven, until everything is golden and crisp and the squash is tender. Remove from the oven and leave in the tray for 5 minutes, then transfer to a serving bowl. While the squash is cooking, pick the pomegranate seeds, removing the pith.

When you are ready to serve, crumble the feta in with the squash, then scatter in the rocket and the pomegranate seeds. Add the red wine vinegar, season generously and gently toss it all together.

V

Sokolatopita: chocolate party cake
Afternoon chamomile and honey cake
Greek coffee-walnut layer cake
Galatopita: golden filo custard pie

Double negative — a mess in two parts

- Meringues
- Rose and strawberry Cretan mess
- Apricot and orange blossom mess

Wine-poached nectarines with anise
Feta, cherry and white chocolate cookies
Ekmek pie
Metaxa 'n' raisin ice cream
Olive oil ice cream slice
Apricot and honey sorbet

Baklava, a love story and inspiration

Baklava buns
Baklava ricotta semifreddo
Baklava cake
Baklava cheesecake, I love you

Yamas! Cheers!

Rizogalo: chilled cinnamon and rose rice pudding
A jug of rizogalo on ice
Ginger lemonade
Cucumber and thyme lemonáda
Frappé crema
A fancy coffee mousse
Oregano, lemon and honey tea
Mastiharita

Sweet
tooth

Sokolatopita: *chocolate party cake*

V

This chocolate traybake looks like any other, right? Not right. It's Greek, which only means one thing: it's drenched in syrup. Before you roll your eyes at the Greek compulsion to drizzle cakes in syrup, let me tell you something: most simple chocolate sponges dry out so quickly. I've only ever met one cocoa sponge that I love and it is made with olive oil instead of butter, which keeps it moist. Otherwise, I think most chocolate sponges taste stale by the next day. This cake, however, is not only fantastically easy, but stays beautifully moist for days — in fact, five whole days by my count. There is less sugar in the cake itself, so the sweetness is balanced out; honestly, you can't really tell it has a syrup. It's not sticky, but rather gives the sponge the most velvety texture. It's the perfect cake for a party; kids and adults love the retro look, and even with the ganache icing it's a breeze to make.

SERVES 12

375g caster sugar
1 cinnamon stick
50ml brandy
125g unsalted butter, plus extra
  for the tray
250g dark and milk chocolate
  (I like half and half)
3 large eggs
175g plain flour
75g cocoa powder
1 teaspoon baking powder
½ teaspoon bicarbonate of soda
½ teaspoon fine sea salt
200ml whole milk
250ml double cream
Sprinkles or fruit (optional)

Place 175g of the caster sugar in a small saucepan with the cinnamon stick, brandy and 150ml of water. Bring to the boil over a medium heat, then simmer for 5 minutes until syrupy. Leave to cool.

Preheat your oven to 190°C/170°C fan/gas mark 5. Grease a deep 30cm × 20cm tray. Melt the butter in a small pan or microwave. Finely chop the chocolate, then set aside. Place the eggs in the bowl of a stand mixer and whisk on a medium speed with the remaining 200g of caster sugar. After a minute, increase the speed to high and whisk for 4 minutes, until pale and voluminous.

Meanwhile, in a separate mixing bowl, whisk together the plain flour, cocoa powder, baking powder, bicarbonate of soda and fine sea salt. When the eggs are ready, whisk in the milk and melted butter, then fold in the dry ingredients and 50g of the chopped chocolate. Pour the batter into the prepared tray and bake in the oven for 25-30 minutes, or until just cooked through. When a skewer inserted into the cake comes out clean, it is done. Remove from the oven and poke holes all over the sponge and evenly drizzle over the cooled syrup. Leave the cake to cool in the tin.

To make the ganache, place the remaining 200g of chopped chocolate in a heatproof bowl. Heat the double cream until it is hot, but not boiling. Immediately pour the cream over the chocolate, leave for 30 seconds, then slowly stir until smooth. Leave to cool for 10 minutes then spread over the cake. Serve as it is or topped with sprinkles or fruit.

Afternoon chamomile and honey cake

Chamomile is one of the most popular herbal teas in Greece, so making it into a soothing, honey-laced cake felt like a journey I wanted to take. And what a journey it was. It took a lot of testing to get here, but now I present the most effortless bake in this chapter. It truly is simple and comforting, while being quietly alluring — good luck having just one slice.

SERVES 8–10

150ml olive oil, plus extra for
 the tin
2 pure chamomile tea bags
1 lemon
175g plain flour
150g ground almonds
100g light soft brown sugar
1½ teaspoons baking powder
½ teaspoon bicarbonate of soda
½ teaspoon fine sea salt
175ml honey
3 large eggs

Preheat your oven to 180°C/160°C fan/gas mark 4. Grease and line a 900g loaf tin with greaseproof paper. Tear open the chamomile tea bags and tip the flowers into a mug and finely grate in the zest of the lemon. Top with 100ml of just-boiled water and leave to brew for 5 minutes.

In a large mixing bowl, whisk together the plain flour, ground almonds, light soft brown sugar, baking powder, bicarbonate of soda and sea salt. In a large measuring jug whisk together the olive oil and 125ml of the honey. Whisk in the eggs. Stir the wet ingredients into the dry, being careful not to over-mix, so that it all just comes together. Stir in the chamomile tea (flowers and all). Pour into the prepared tin and bake for 55–60 minutes, or until golden and just cooked through. It's done when a skewer inserted into the middle of the cake comes out clean.

When the cake is ready, remove from the oven, lightly prick all over with a skewer and drizzle with the remaining 50ml of honey. Leave in the tin to cool completely before serving.

V + DF

Greek coffee–walnut layer cake

V

Karydopita is a hugely popular cake all around Greece, and despite being eaten year-round it has an almost festive, Christmassy feel. It is made with barely any flour, using mostly ground walnuts and breadcrumbs, and is soaked with a spiced syrup to create a dense, sticky texture. Although I enjoy the traditional version, it is quite rich. I wanted to create something that felt like the love child of karydopita but with the lightness of an English coffee–walnut cake. This beauty is just that. It is fancy enough for special occasions, but familiar enough to feel at home for afternoon tea. I use barely whipped double cream between the layers, as I don't think it needs much more. If you want to make it more of a showstopper, then feel free to increase the cream quantity or make a light buttercream.

SERVES 8–12

250g butter, plus extra for the tin
400g walnuts
300g caster sugar
6 large eggs
100g breadcrumbs
50g plain flour
2 ½ teaspoons baking powder
½ teaspoon bicarbonate of soda
2 teaspoons ground cinnamon,
 plus extra to serve (optional)
90ml brandy
½ teaspoon fine sea salt
200ml coffee
300ml double cream
Icing sugar, to serve (optional)

Preheat your oven to 190°C/170°C fan/gas mark 5. Butter and use greaseproof paper to line the base of two 20cm springform cake tins. Spread the walnuts out on a baking tray and roast for 8–10 minutes, until darker golden, then remove and leave to cool. Place in a food processor and blitz till fine. Pulse in the butter and 200g of the caster sugar until you have a pale and creamy mixture. Scoop this into a large mixing bowl. Separate the eggs and beat the yolks into the walnut-butter mixture, one at a time. Stir in the breadcrumbs, plain flour, baking powder, bicarbonate of soda and ground cinnamon. Stir in the brandy, then leave to one side.

In the bowl of a stand mixer, beat the egg whites and the sea salt until they form soft peaks. Using a large metal spoon, fold in one spoonful of the egg whites to loosen the walnut mixture, then fold in the rest, keeping in as much air as possible. Divide the mixture between the prepared tins and bake for 30–35 minutes, until cooked through. A skewer inserted in the middle of the cake should come out clean. Leave to cool in the tins for 10 minutes, then turn out onto a wire rack to cool completely.

When the cakes are cool, place the remaining 100g of caster sugar in a small pan with the coffee and bring to the boil. Leave to bubble away for 6–8 minutes until you have a lovely thickened syrup. Whip the double cream to loose folds in a large bowl. Cut the cakes in half horizontally. Place one cake on a board or stand and evenly brush with a third of the syrup. Spread with a third of the cream and top with another cake. Repeat with the remaining syrup, cream and cakes. Serve as is, or dusted with icing sugar and a little ground cinnamon, if you like.

Galatopita: *golden filo custard pie*

The direct translation of this dish is 'milk pie', which is quite pleasing and a good indicator of the balance I was looking to achieve here. This recipe is the right level of cream v syrup for me. Sweet, but not a smack-in-the-face sugar hit. Creamy without feeling like you are downing a pint of the rich stuff. A milk pie, rather than a cream pie. There is a version of galatopita which has no filo, but I prefer this one. If you find using filo pastry intimidating, I urge you to give this a try — it is a very forgiving recipe and can take any cracks or misshapen sheets. And custard and syrup help cover a multitude of sins. Finally, you must leave it to cool completely before serving. It's torture, I know...

SERVES 9

8 cardamom pods (or a good
  sprinkling of ground cinnamon
  or grated lemon zest)
300g caster sugar
A pinch of saffron (optional)
100g unsalted butter
250g filo
3 large eggs
2 teaspoons vanilla extract
A pinch of fine sea salt
200ml whole milk
200ml double cream

Crush the cardamom pods a little. Make a sugar syrup by placing 175g of the sugar in a saucepan with 125ml of water and the crushed cardamom and saffron, if using. Bring to the boil then simmer on a medium heat for 5 minutes. Take off the heat and set aside to cool.

Preheat your oven to 190°C/170°C fan/gas mark 5. Melt the butter. Use a little of it to butter a 24cm square or round cake tin. Cover the filo with a slightly damp tea towel, then, one by one, brush each sheet with butter and concertina the sheet lengthwise. Start by rolling the first sheet into a rose in the centre of the cake tin. Continue building the concertina filo around the centre rose like a snail. Brush with the remaining butter and pop in the oven for 20-25 minutes, until deep golden all over.

Whisk the remaining 125g of sugar with the eggs, vanilla extract and salt. Slowly whisk in the milk and cream until smooth. When the filo is ready, pour over the custard, jiggling the pan to encourage it into all the folds, and return to the oven. Bake for 18-20 minutes, or until just set. Prick all over with a sharp knife and pour over the cooled sugar syrup. Leave to cool completely before serving.

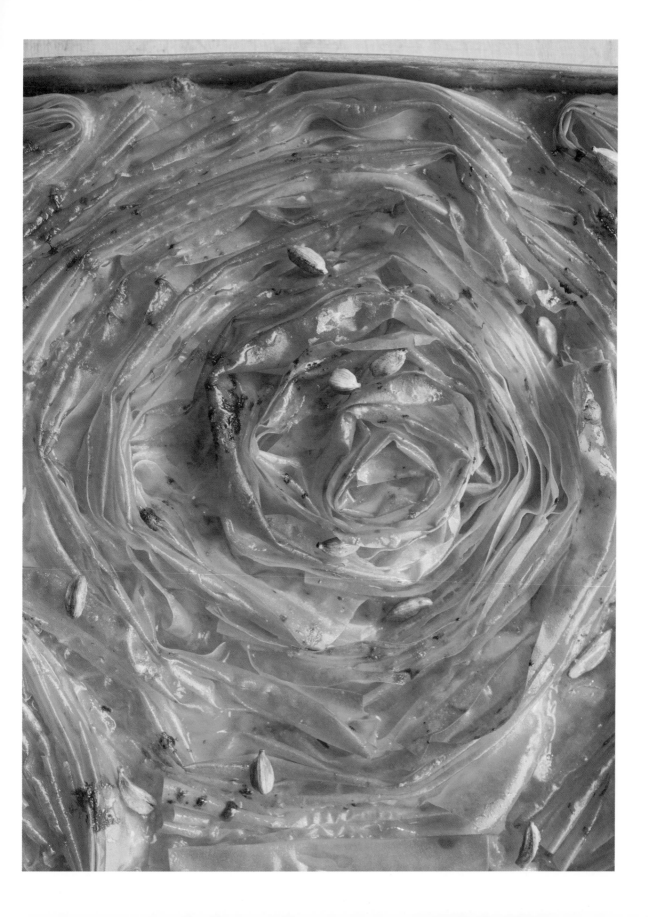

Double negative — a mess in two parts

Eton mess is probably my biggest food contradiction. Aesthetically, I appreciate those piles of billowy, rippled meringues you see in bakery windows, but you will never find me nibbling on one. The sweetness and texture, literally and metaphorically, set my teeth on edge. Even writing about them is making me feel weird. I'm also not a big fan of whipped cream, much to the dismay of my mum, who is completely addicted to the stuff — with desserts, on cakes, in life. In the late 80s, my maternal grandparents would occasionally take us to McDonald's for breakfast as a treat. Polystyrene boxes with rubbery pancakes and sausage patties will forever have a soft spot in my heart. Little plastic tubs filled with a syrup that had probably never been in the same postcode as a maple tree. And there was Mum with a can of squirty cream in her handbag to have over the pancakes. Every single time.

Here is the anomaly with my hate for meringues and whipped cream: put them together and you have one of my favourite puddings of all time. It's the dessert version of a double negative — two wrongs that most definitely make a right. The crisp sweetness and soft cream balance has to be spot on, and there must be a good amount of fruit, but when it is good, just pass me the whole bowl and a spoon, because I am all in.

Meringues

V + GF

This is my best meringue recipe. You don't have to use cream of tartar. I think that it makes the meringues more stable, more reliable — and I find there's a nicer chew in the middle when I use it — but this recipe will still work fine without.

MAKES 4

2 large egg whites
120g caster sugar
¼ teaspoon cream of tartar
 (optional)

Preheat your oven 140°C/120°C fan/gas mark 1. Place the egg whites in the bowl of a stand mixer. The bowl must be very clean, or the egg whites will not whisk up properly. Whisk on high until soft peaks form, then, with the motor still running, gradually add the caster sugar, one spoonful at a time, waiting until each has been fully incorporated before adding the next. Add the cream of tartar, if using. Once all the sugar has been added, keep the mixer on for 5 minutes, until you have a glossy smooth meringue and stiff peaks have formed. Rub a little of the mixture between your fingers; you shouldn't be able to feel a grain of sugar.

Line a baking sheet with greaseproof paper (you can stick it in place with a few dots of meringue) and spoon the meringue into four discs. Don't pile them too high, as you want them to be fairly well cooked through, and they don't have to be perfect, as you are going to crush them. Bake for 1 hour and 15-30 minutes, until firm and quite crisp underneath, but still (hopefully) chewy in the centre. Turn off the oven, open the door a fraction, and leave to cool in there before using.

Rose and strawberry Cretan mess

V + GF

I don't think I'll ever eat rose-flavoured loukoumi (Turkish delight) without flashbacks of my childhood and attempting to read *The Lion, the Witch and the Wardrobe* (I'm not entirely convinced I actually ever finished it). It's a sweet that feels magical and mystical. The addition of yoghurt does help make this lighter and less rich than traditional Eton mess, though the choice to use it is nothing to do with gluttony — I just prefer it this way. The yoghurt's tang cuts through the sweetness of the meringue perfectly.

SERVES 6

600g strawberries
3 tablespoons honey
100g rose loukoumi (Turkish delight)
300ml double cream
300g Greek yoghurt
1–2 tablespoons rose water
140g meringues (see page 225 for a recipe, or use shop-bought)
A handful of pistachios

Hull and roughly chop the strawberries. Place them in a bowl, stir in two tablespoons of the honey and leave to one side. Chop or snip the loukoumi as best you can into 1cm pieces; they'll be sticky but don't worry about being too perfect.

Whip the cream in a large mixing bowl till you have soft peaks — they should just hold and leave a trail. Fold through the Greek yoghurt and then the rose water, a half-tablespoon at a time, tasting as you go. Break in the meringue — you don't want it too fine or it will disintegrate. Add most of the chopped loukoumi, strawberries and honeyed juices and stir through only enough to just combine. Have a taste and add a little extra honey, if you like. Roughly chop the pistachios. Finish by drizzling with any leftover honey-strawberry juices, then top with the reserved strawberries and loukoumi, and scatter over the pistachios.

Apricot and orange blossom mess

Any time I make a dessert with apricot and orange blossom (it happens a lot), my sister says 'you *are* apricot and orange blossom', as if this heavenly combination is also my flavour profile. I take this as a compliment. Thank you, Lulu, for your repeated observation on how obsessed I am with this pairing. I could hardly leave it out of the book, could I?

SERVES 6

600g apricots
½ lemon
80g caster sugar
300ml double cream
300g Greek yoghurt
1–2 tablespoons orange blossom
 water
4 tablespoons honey
140g meringues (see page 225 for
 a recipe, or use shop-bought)
A handful of pistachios

Preheat your oven to 200°C/180°C fan/gas mark 6. Halve and stone the apricots, then roughly chop the flesh. Place them all in a roasting tray to fit snugly, and finely grate in the lemon zest. Squeeze in the lemon juice and toss with the caster sugar. Place in the oven and roast for 30 minutes, until the fruit softens and starts to caramelise slightly. Remove from the oven, lightly mash with a fork so you have a rough purée and set aside to cool.

When the apricots are cool, whip the double cream in a large mixing bowl till you have soft peaks — they should just hold and leave a trail. Fold through the Greek yoghurt and orange blossom water, a half-tablespoon at a time to taste. Drizzle in the honey and break in the meringue — you don't want it too fine or it will disintegrate. Stir in the roasted apricots, being careful not to over-mix it; you want to just swirl everything together. Roughly chop the pistachios and scatter over the top before serving.

V + GF

Wine-poached nectarines with anise

VG + GF

I love poaching nectarines in a sweet wine from the island of Samos, and adding the merest hint of anise elevates it to be an elegant, fuss-free, peak summertime dessert. I appreciate that expecting people to source this very particular wine is probably not realistic, so I've written the recipe to work for any table — not sweet — white or rosé wine. Make it ahead, chill, then serve cold. Have bowls of sweetened cream or Greek yoghurt to pass round, and scatter over a few edible flowers if you're feeling particularly fabulous.

SERVES 4

4 ripe nectarines — I prefer white ones but yellow are nice, too
500ml white or rosé wine
250g caster sugar
2 pinches of anise seeds
½ lemon

Start by peeling the nectarines. Score a little 'x' on the top, where the stalk would be, and plunge them into just-boiled water for 30 seconds (the same method for peeling tomatoes). You should see the skin start to curl away. Transfer to a bowl of ice-cold water and peel off the skins — they should come off easily.

Place the wine, caster sugar and anise seeds in a medium saucepan on a medium heat. Add a couple of strips of lemon zest, and squeeze in the juice. Don't bring to the boil, but heat just enough so that the sugar dissolves. Carefully put the nectarines in the pan and leave to simmer away for 10-12 minutes, until just cooked through — don't let them become mushy. You'll need to turn them a couple of times to cook evenly.

When the nectarines are ready, remove from the pan and leave to one side. Turn up the heat and bring the remaining liquid to the boil. Leave to bubble away for 5-8 minutes, until thickened and a little syrupy. Let the syrup cool completely and pour over the nectarines. Chill and leave covered in the fridge until ready to serve.

Feta, cherry and white chocolate cookies

V

I am obsessed with these cookies, as you should be. Are you the kind of person who likes to offer your friends new bakes and say, rather hysterically, 'but you'll *never* guess what's in it. No, seriously, go on, have a guess!', all the while getting a bit too close to the poor person, knowing they probably won't guess correctly? (You hope they won't, otherwise they've just killed the punchline.) Is that you? You are my people; read on.

Putting feta in sweets isn't a new thing (check out my baklava cheesecake on page 250), and many Greeks and Cypriots regularly sweeten soft cheeses for biscuits and cakes. Putting feta in scones and muffins set me on a path, playing with textures and flavours in cookies. The feta isn't in there for shock value; it adds the salty edge that really lifts these biscuits. Sweet, chewy, tart, salty... I'll stop raving — just promise to make them.

MAKES 12

160g unsalted butter
100g white chocolate
125g light soft brown sugar
125g caster sugar
1 large egg
275g plain flour
½ teaspoon baking powder
½ teaspoon fine sea salt
100g feta
75g dried cherries, sour if possible,
  or dried cranberries

Cut the butter into cubes and add to a small pan over a medium heat. Melt the butter, then take it a little further so it turns golden-brown and starts to smell nutty. You'll see little flecks of brown, toasted butter solids at the bottom of the pan. Meanwhile, chop the white chocolate and place in a large mixing bowl. Pour over the melted butter, leave for a minute, then stir until smooth. Beat in both types of sugar with a wooden spoon. Beat in the egg.

In a separate bowl, whisk the flour, baking powder and fine sea salt together. Add to the chocolate mixture and stir until it all just comes together. Crumble in the feta, add the dried cherries and mix briefly. Line two baking trays with greaseproof paper and shape the cookie mixture into 12 even-sized balls. (Not to be a geek, but I weigh the dough and divide by 12. You're looking at 80-85g per cookie.) Place on the trays, and make sure there is plenty of room between them. Place the trays in the fridge for at least 1 hour to help the mixture firm up so the cookies don't spread too fast — the longer you leave them the more domed and chewy they will be.

Preheat the oven to 200°C/180°C fan/gas mark 6 and bake the cookies for 18 minutes, until deep golden-brown at the edge. If you have chilled the dough overnight, they might need a minute or two longer. Leave the cookies to cool completely on their trays before serving or storing in an airtight container.

Ekmek pie

Some recipes I mess around with, twist and make my own. Others I leave intact, bowing to their glory and knowing that they are perfect just the way they are. Ekmek is one of those. Ekmek really isn't right if it is made fancy, or in something other than a Pyrex dish (I'd allow an enamel tray, too). That's not to say I won't go off-piste one day, but for now, here is a classic. This is yiayia-style home cooking — big spoons, unfrilly and delicious.

SERVES 8-10

200g kataifi pastry
100g unsalted butter
350g caster sugar
½ lemon
900ml whole milk
4 large egg yolks
80g cornflour
2 tablespoons orange
 blossom water
400ml double cream
50g pistachios

Preheat your oven to 200°C/180°C fan/gas mark 6. Tease out the kataifi and drape in a large roasting tin. Melt 60g of the butter and toss through the pastry, then place the tin in the oven. Bake for 40-45 minutes, until crisp and golden all over. When it is ready, leave to cool a little, then break the kataifi up and evenly spread into a 30cm x 24cm dish or tray.

Place 200g of the caster sugar in a small pan with a couple of strips of lemon zest and 250ml of water. Bring to the boil, then leave to bubble away gently for 4-5 minutes, until reduced and thickened but not coloured. Evenly spoon the hot syrup over the cool kataifi and set aside.

Warm the milk in a large pan. Meanwhile, in a large mixing bowl, whisk the remaining 150g of caster sugar with the egg yolks until smooth and pale. Whisk in the cornflour. When the milk is hot but not boiling, slowly ladle a little into the egg mixture, whisking constantly until smooth and loosened — you want to be really careful not to scramble the egg mixture. Then pour the mixture into the saucepan with the rest of the hot milk, whisking all the while. Reduce the heat a little, and keep whisking until everything is thickened, creamy and smooth. Remove from the heat, add the orange blossom water and dot in the remaining 40g of the butter, and keep whisking. Pour the custard into the kataifi pastry-lined tin and leave to one side to cool completely. When cool, refrigerate until needed.

When you are ready to serve the ekmek, gently whip the double cream to soft folds and spoon over the pie. Finely chop the pistachios and sprinkle over just before serving.

Metaxa 'n' raisin ice cream

V

Metaxa is a spirit made in Samos from muscat grapes. It has a deep, smooth aroma and taste; it's most similar to brandy, but it's distilled with botanicals, including rose. No wonder I love it. Here, I've used it in a riff on the classic rum 'n' raisin ice cream. I love using my ice cream machine, but I also love the ease of no-churn recipes: no eggs, no custard making, straight into the freezer it goes. You can find Metaxa in some UK supermarkets, or you can substitute with brandy, if you must. What you absolutely can't substitute is the Greek yoghurt; it has to be full-fat. In fact, check the brands available to you and buy the one with the highest fat content.

This has a lot going on flavour-wise, so I like it best served as is. However, you can try it affogato-style, with hot coffee over the top, perhaps with a little butter biscuit on the side. It would also work at a barbecue with some grilled fruit.

SERVES 8–10

250g raisins
40g light soft brown sugar
125ml Metaxa, or brandy
300g full-fat Greek yoghurt
1 teaspoon vanilla extract
½ orange
A pinch of fine sea salt
100g icing sugar
250ml double cream

Roughly chop half of the raisins. Add them to a small saucepan with the remaining whole raisins, the light soft brown sugar and Metaxa. Stir together and place on a medium heat. Heat through, stirring occasionally, until the Metaxa just begins to boil, then remove from the heat. Leave to cool for 45 minutes, so that the raisins absorb all the liquid. Make sure to stir them occasionally, so they all have a chance to get juicy.

When the raisins have cooled, mix together the Greek yoghurt with the vanilla, the finely grated zest of the orange and the sea salt. Sift in the icing sugar and stir till loosened. Whip the double cream to soft peaks, then fold in the yoghurt until well combined. Ripple in the cooled raisins and spoon into a container with a tight-fitting lid. Smooth out the top of the cream, seal and place in the freezer. Ideally leave to freeze overnight, or for at least 8 hours, before serving.

Olive oil ice cream slice

Olive oil ice cream is a glorious thing; it has a satiny texture and a subtle flavour. Huge fan. You can make the ice cream and stop there, if you like, but ice cream sandwiches always get people excited. I've used a classic Greek biscuit that is a bit like a Rich Tea: simple and doesn't complicate the flavours. However, use whatever you can, preferably something similar, simple and rectangular if possible, for maximum effect.

SERVES 8

400ml double cream
200ml whole milk
3 large egg yolks
175g caster sugar
A pinch of fine sea salt
3 tablespoons extra virgin olive oil
16 pti-ber (petit beurre) Greek morning biscuits, or other simple rectangular biscuit
8 teaspoons fine-cut marmalade

Pour the cream and milk into a medium saucepan and warm over a medium heat. Whisk the egg yolks with the caster sugar and sea salt in a large mixing bowl until pale and smooth. When the milk mixture is hot but not boiling, ladle some of it into the egg mixture, whisking the whole time so it doesn't scramble the eggs. When you have added enough milk to loosen the eggs, pour everything back into the pan. Cook on a medium heat, whisking constantly, to thicken the mixture. You are looking for a custard that is thick enough to coat the back of a spoon. As soon as it is ready, pour into a clean mixing bowl to cool quickly. If you are worried about lumps, you can strain it. When it is cold, cover and chill in the fridge for at least 6 hours, overnight if possible.

When the custard is ready to churn, whisk in the extra virgin olive oil. I like to use a stick blender to really emulsify it thoroughly. Pour into your ice cream machine and churn according to the machine instructions. When it is ready, get your tub prepared. Line a 25cm x 18cm container or dish with clingfilm. This size is based on using the Greek biscuits I use, but if you are using other biscuits, just make sure the dish is big enough to line with eight biscuits (two rows of four). Place eight biscuits on the base, printed-side down. Spread over the ice cream. Spread the underside of the remaining biscuits with marmalade, then press them, marmalade-side down, on top, aligned as best you can with the base biscuits, and cover the container with the lid or more clingfilm. Place in the freezer for at least an hour to firm up before serving.

When you're ready, turn the frozen slab out on a chopping board and cut along the edges of the biscuits into eight blocks. Serve wrapped in a bit of greaseproof paper for ultimate retro vibes.

Apricot and honey sorbet

I've previously mentioned my love of apricots. One of the first things we planted in our small London garden was an apricot tree. It took a few years to get a bumper season, but now it's in full swing. In early summer, I go out daily to check on them, get unreasonably cross when one of the girls yanks one off the tree before its time, and spend my days planning how I will honour them when they are ready. Some will be eaten immediately, standing by the tree. Some with halloumi (page 68). This sorbet is third on the list.

SERVES 4-6

500g apricots
150g caster sugar
50g honey (agave syrup, if making it vegan)
½ lemon

Halve and stone the apricots, then cut in half again. If you can, crack open a couple of the stones with a nutcracker (or use a pestle and mortar) and remove the almond-like kernel in the middle. Place the caster sugar in a large saucepan with the honey and 400ml of water and the apricot kernels, if using. Bring to the boil on a medium-high heat and then add the chopped apricots. Simmer for 5–8 minutes, until the apricots start to soften. Remove from the heat. Leave the apricots to cool before blitzing in a blender, then strain through a fine sieve into a large bowl or jug. Stir in one tablespoon of lemon juice, and chill in the fridge for at least 6 hours.

When the mixture is ready, churn in an ice cream maker (according to the manufacturer's instructions) until you have a silky, pastel-coloured sorbet. Store in an airtight container in your freezer until needed.

Baklava, a love story and inspiration

I think the best type of love grows slowly. It's a deeper appreciation that builds over time rather than a hedonistic, smack-in-the-face flash (that kind is fun, but usually fleeting). My love of baklava is one of those slow loves. Baklava has been a constant in my life since I was small. I'd often be given small pieces after a meal or during a visit to someone's house. But I never 'loved' it. I found it too sweet and so I gave up on it.

Then I decided to start playing around with the recipe myself. I ate different kinds and started to seek it out, and broadened my appreciation. I started to twist the base flavours into new recipes, which I really enjoyed. Now, you can't even mention the 'B' word without me interrupting you. Baklava ice cream, you say? I'm making a beeline. Baklava cheesecake? My most favourite of all my favourite desserts. This sub-chapter is a homage to nuts and syrup, to cinnamon and butter, to honey and filo — to all the elements that make up my new and deepest sweet love.

Baklava buns

A cinnamon bun but make it baklava-themed with two topping options... A lot to love here. If you prefer a simple bun, opt for the glaze. If you like a full-on frosting situation, you won't regret the tahini cream cheese option (also a dream on the sokolatopita, page 216).

MAKES 9

280g light soft brown sugar
1 × 7g sachet of fact-action dried yeast
500g strong bread flour, plus extra for dusting
¾ teaspoon ground cinnamon
¾ teaspoon fine sea salt
2 tablespoons olive oil
100g walnuts
75g unsalted butter, at room temperature, plus extra for the tin

Orange glaze
1 orange
175g caster sugar

Tahini cream cheese frosting
50g unsalted butter, at room temperature
3 tablespoons tahini
175g icing sugar
150g cream cheese

Place 50g of the soft brown sugar in a jug with 270ml of warm water, then whisk in the yeast. Leave to one side. In a large bowl, or a stand mixer, whisk together the bread flour, ½ teaspoon of the cinnamon and the salt. Make a well and pour in the yeast mixture and olive oil. Mix it all together well and knead the dough until smooth and elastic (by hand or with a dough hook). Transfer to a clean bowl, cover with a tea towel and leave in a warm spot for 2 hours, or until doubled in size.

While the dough rises, prepare the topping of your choice. For the glaze, finely grate the orange zest into a pan and squeeze in the juice. Add the caster sugar and 200ml of water and bring to a boil, swirling occasionally, to melt the sugar. Boil for about 5 minutes to thicken, then set aside. For the frosting, beat the butter and tahini until smooth. Sift in the icing sugar, then beat in the cream cheese until just combined — do not over-mix, or the texture will thin. Set aside until needed.

Roughly chop the walnuts and toast in a frying pan until they start to smell nutty and darken a little. Sprinkle in 30g of the soft brown sugar and the remaining ¼ teaspoon of cinnamon. Stir quickly for 30 seconds then remove from the heat. Tip out on a board to cool, then chop up a little more. When the dough is ready, knock it back onto a clean surface dusted with flour and roll into a rectangle, about 40cm × 25cm. Spread with the butter, and sprinkle with the remaining 200g of brown sugar and all the walnut mixture. Pat into the dough, then roll into a log, starting at the longer side. Cut into nine pieces. Butter a 23cm square cake or roasting tin and put the buns in, cut-side up. Leave to prove for a further 20 minutes. Preheat the oven to 200°C/180°C fan/gas mark 6.

When the buns are risen, just about touching, bake for 20-25 minutes, until golden and cooked through. As soon as the buns come out the oven, either drizzle over the cooled syrup or ice with the frosting. Leave the buns to cool in the tin before eating.

V

Baklava ricotta semifreddo

V

I'd say this ice cream is more of a pudding than one for scooping on a cone (though by all means). Take it out of the freezer a good 30 minutes before you want to serve it and turn it out of its loaf tin onto a serving board. The caramelised filo bottom becomes the attractive top, and you can scatter with more nuts if you like, or even a drizzle of honey. The texture the filo gets in the freezer is so pleasing — much of it remains crunchy but some bits soften to become chewy and it's just marvellous, every part.

SERVES 10

70g unsalted butter
½ teaspoon ground cinnamon
100g caster sugar
6 sheets of filo
75g walnuts
500g ricotta
1 tablespoon rose water
400ml double cream
1 lemon
100g honey

Preheat your oven to 200°C/180°C fan/gas mark 6. Melt the butter. Mix the ground cinnamon with 40g of the caster sugar. Brush the filo sheets with the butter, one by one, and sprinkle each with one-sixth of the cinnamon-sugar mixture. Scrunch each sheet into waves or loose rosettes in a baking tray. Finely chop the walnuts and scatter over the top. Place in the oven and bake for 20 minutes, until crisp and golden-brown all over. Remove and leave to cool.

When the filo and nuts are cool, scrunch it all up in the tray so you have a mixture of medium and small pieces to stir into the ice cream; it's nice if some bits are clumpy. Line a 900g loaf tin with clingfilm; leave the edges long so you can fold them back over the filling. Sprinkle in enough filo mixture to cover the bottom of the tin. Blitz the ricotta, the remaining 60g of caster sugar and the rose water in a food processor until just combined and glossy. Whip the cream in a large mixing bowl until soft peaks form and then fold in the ricotta mixture. Finely grate in the lemon zest and drizzle in the honey. Fold most of the remaining filo into the cream mixture. Spoon the ice cream mixture into the prepared loaf tin, fold over the clingfilm and press gently on top, then freeze for at least 6 hours before serving.

To serve, bring out of the freezer and leave at room temperature for 30 minutes. Turn out the ice cream loaf on a board, scatter with the reserved toasted and crushed filo, and serve in slices.

Baklava cake

V + DF

I love how striking this cake is. You can thank social media for the origins of this idea, however, I have had a play, and made it even more baklava-like, if that is possible. Do not be put off by the slightly longer than average (for me) ingredients list, as it is pretty easy to throw together. You'll see I've instructed for three rounds of honey, but I think it can take it, as it isn't the sweetest cake. It is such a great afternoon bake, perfect with an intense Greek coffee. Or serve a slice with a dollop of the tangiest Greek yoghurt, a drizzle of sticky (orange blossom if you can) honey, and you've got a dream dessert right there.

SERVES 12

120ml olive oil, plus extra for
 the tin
100g nuts — I like a mix of
 walnuts and pistachios
1 teaspoon ground cinnamon
½ teaspoon fine sea salt
120g honey, plus extra to serve
225g caster sugar
3 large eggs
125ml orange juice
1 tablespoon rose water (if you do
 not have, or like, rose water, then
 use the finely grated zest of an
 orange)
200g fine semolina
135g self-raising flour

Preheat your oven to 190°C/170°C fan/gas mark 5. Grease a 20cm springform cake tin with a little olive oil and line the base with baking paper. Chop the nuts, so they are small but not too fine. Place in a large bowl with half of the ground cinnamon and half of the fine sea salt. Stir in 60g of the honey and 25g of the caster sugar. Mix together well, then spoon into the base of the tin and press out evenly. Pop in the fridge.

Place the eggs and remaining 200g of caster sugar in the bowl of a stand mixer, and whisk for 5 minutes until pale and light. (You can also do this in a large mixing bowl with an electric hand whisk.) Whisk in the orange juice, olive oil and rose water. Whisk together the fine semolina and self-raising flour with the remaining ground cinnamon and fine sea salt. Fold into the egg mixture with a large metal spoon (this will help keep it as light as possible), but mix it well enough so that there are no flour pockets. Pour the cake mixture into the nut and honey-lined tin. Place the filled cake tin on a baking sheet, to catch any honey that oozes out. Bake for 50-60 minutes, until golden and cooked (a skewer inserted into the middle should come out clean).

When done, run a knife around the inside of the tin, to loosen the cake from the sides. Leave it in the tin for 3 minutes, then turn out on a wire rack. Carefully remove the tin and peel off the baking paper. Drizzle with the remaining 60g of honey and leave to cool completely. Slice and serve with a dollop of Greek yoghurt and more honey if you like (I like).

Baklava cheesecake, I love you

Look, I don't want to gush too much about this recipe, but I must. I'm obsessed. It combines all my favourite flavours (honey, nuts, rose, cinnamon) and textures (crunchy, creamy, chewy). And it looks so great. I'll never forget the first time I made it and presented it to my family, my harshest critics. First there were intrigued looks, then lots of nodding. My yiayia, usually the first to dish out constructive criticism, was speechless — she had nothing. Nothing but smiles. That was it, that was when I knew I'd hit peak baklava.

SERVES 12

225g caster sugar
1 lemon
1 tablespoon rose water
60g unsalted butter
100g walnuts
1 teaspoon ground cinnamon
250g filo
200g white chocolate
200g feta
280g full-fat cream cheese
200ml double cream
About 3 tablespoons honey
Chopped pistachios, to serve

V

First, make a syrup. Place 100g of the caster sugar in a small saucepan with 125ml of water and two strips of lemon zest (use a peeler for this). Bring to the boil on a medium heat, swirl to dissolve the sugar, then reduce the heat a little. Simmer for 5-8 minutes, until you have a thick, but not coloured syrup. Stir in the rose water and leave to cool completely.

Preheat your oven to 200°C/180°C fan/gas mark 6. Grease a 20cm springform cake tin with a little of the butter. Place the walnuts in a dry frying pan and toast for a few minutes on a medium heat. Once they start to smell nutty, stir in the ground cinnamon and 25g of the caster sugar. Let the sugar caramelise slightly, then tip the nuts out onto a chopping board. When they're cool enough to handle, finely chop.

Melt the rest of the butter in a small pan. Lay two sheets of filo over the cake tin, overlapping slightly, so they completely cover the base and sides, then brush all over with the melted butter. Sprinkle a quarter of the chopped walnuts over the bottom, and repeat the process twice more with filo then butter and walnuts (keep the remaining walnuts aside). Top with a final layer of filo, really push it in to the bottom and sides, then brush with butter. Trim off any excess pastry around the top with scissors and bake in the oven for 25-30 minutes, until crisp and golden.

When the filo shell is ready, remove from the oven and drizzle the cold syrup over the hot pastry, particularly down the sides. Leave to cool.

(Recipe continued overleaf)

(Recipe continues)

For the cheesecake filling, break the white chocolate into small, even pieces and place in a heatproof bowl. Either melt in a microwave or over a pan of simmering water — be careful that the bowl doesn't touch the water in the pan or the chocolate will seize up. Stir occasionally until the chocolate is just melted.

Meanwhile, break the feta into pieces into a large bowl. Add the remaining 100g of caster sugar and blitz with a stick blender till smooth. Add the cream cheese and finely grate in the remaining lemon zest. Beat with a whisk, not a stick blender, until smooth (electric beaters would be best if you can handle more washing up). Add the double cream, whisk until light and then finally stir in the melted white chocolate.

Spoon the filling into the baked and cooled filo case, loosely cover and chill in the fridge for at least 4 hours, overnight if possible. Just before serving, drizzle with a little honey and scatter over the reserved walnuts, and some chopped pistachios for a pop of colour.

Rizogalo: *chilled cinnamon and rose rice pudding*

This is a classic recipe and I don't mess around with it, aside from occasionally adding a little cardamom, as it complements the rose and cinnamon. Purists can leave it out.

SERVES 4-6

250g pudding rice
750ml whole milk
180g caster sugar
4 cardamom pods (optional)
300ml single cream
2 tablespoon rose water
2 teaspoons ground cinnamon

Place the pudding rice in a large saucepan. Stir in the milk and sugar. Crush the cardamom pods and grind the seeds. Add the ground seeds to the pan with 300ml of water. Bring to the boil on a high heat, then reduce to low and simmer for 20-25 minutes, stirring occasionally. You are looking for just-cooked rice; it needs to have the slightest bite because it will carry on cooking as it cools. Stir in the cream and rose water and bring back to the boil, then immediately remove from the heat. Decant into serving bowls, sprinkle each bowl with ¼-½ teaspoon of ground cinnamon and leave to cool. Transfer to the fridge, and serve once chilled.

V + GF

A jug of rizogalo on ice

I had to include a recipe for rizogalo. It is a classic in the Greek repertoire, and for my family. However, just quietly down here in the small print, I do not really love it. I do, however, love horchata — or horchata de arroz — a Mexican drink that is made from blitzing rice and cinnamon and soaking it with sugar. It is then strained and served over ice, and is wonderfully refreshing. I've applied the same principle to Greek rizogalo and it is heavenly over ice on a hot, hot day.

You'll need all the same ingredients as above, apart from the single cream. Place the rice in a blender with the sugar, ground cardamom seeds, rose water and ground cinnamon. Add 100ml of cold water and blitz until you have a smooth paste. Add a further 350ml of water and as much of the milk as you can fit in your blender and blitz again. Transfer to a large jug and stir in the remaining milk. Cover and refrigerate overnight to infuse. Strain through a fine-mesh sieve and pour into ice-filled glasses.

(Photo overleaf)

Ginger lemonade

VG + GF

Thessaloniki is a brilliant food city, perhaps my favourite place to eat in Greece. The food culture feels wide-ranging, due to its geography and historically diverse population. One of the most surprising things to me is the use of ginger. In Corfu they make a ginger beer — *tsitsibira* — but I hadn't seen it in a drink anywhere else in Greece before I went to Thessaloniki. There I had it in the form of ground ginger sprinkled over salepi — a thick, creamy warm drink made from white orchid root — that felt particularly nourishing. I also drank a lot of ginger lemonade, which was widely on offer in cafés and bars around town.

SERVES 8-10

A hand of ginger (about 175g)
250g caster sugar
4 lemons
Ice cubes
Very cold soda water

Wash and dry the ginger, then cut into 5mm slices. Place the caster sugar in a small pan with 250ml of water and the sliced ginger. Bring to the boil on a medium heat, then reduce the heat and simmer for 3 minutes, until slightly thickened. Remove from the heat and leave to cool.

Once the syrup is fully cooled, squeeze in the lemon juice and mix in well. Strain into a serving jug and chill for at least an hour. When you're ready to serve, pour a little into a glass, add ice cubes and top up with soda water — I like to have about a third lemonade and two-thirds soda.

(Photo overleaf)

Cucumber and thyme lemonáda

I'll make almost anything into a lemonade — leftover fruit, berries that are too squishy, sweetly fragrant herbs like basil, rosemary or tarragon. This cucumber one is a big hit in our house; my daughters love it, it's refreshing and it's easily turned into a thirst-quenching but classy cocktail by adding a shot of mastiha (my favourite Greek spirit). You could even add a generous splash of sparkling wine with the soda and make a verdant summer spritz.

MAKES 10 GENEROUS DRINKS

1 cucumber
200g caster sugar
6 lemons
½ bunch of thyme
Ice cubes
Very cold soda water
Mastiha liqueur (optional)

Trim the ends of the cucumber and roughly chop. Place in a blender with 200ml of cold water and blitz until smooth. Place a fine-mesh sieve over a large bowl and pour in the cucumber mixture. Leave to strain, giving it a stir and a press to encourage as much liquid out as possible.

Meanwhile, place the caster sugar in a measuring jug and top with 200ml of just-boiled water. Leave for a few minutes, stirring occasionally, to dissolve. Once fully dissolved, squeeze in the lemon juice, discarding any pips, and mix well. Pour into a large serving jug and mix in the strained cucumber juice, then chill until needed.

To serve, mix in the thyme sprigs and a handful of ice cubes. Pour a little into a glass and top up with soda water — I like to have about a third lemonade and two-thirds soda. To make it boozy, add a 50ml shot of mastiha over some ice in a glass before pouring in the lemonade and topping up with soda to taste.

VG + GF

Frappé crema

Greek frappé is the taste of summer holidays for many people, so I'm always surprised people don't make this iced coffee when they get home. It's so easy — coffee, sugar and ice, shaken hard — but I think people assume that to get that thick crema on top you need a special gadget. The only thing you absolutely need is instant coffee; Greek frappé can not be made with espresso. It is thought to have originated in Thessaloniki in 1957 by a Nestlé representative in need of a coffee fix but with no access to hot water. The magic foaming effect made waves more recently on social media via south-east Asia in another form: dalgona coffee. This method gives a much denser, mousse-like foam as you use an electric hand whisk. It also works with decaffeinated instant coffee.

SERVES 2

2 tablespoons instant coffee,
  ideally Nescafé
2 tablespoons caster sugar

Using an electric hand whisk, whip the instant coffee and caster sugar with three tablespoons of boiling water in a mixing bowl for about 5 minutes, until you have a thick mousse. By the time you are done, it will be voluminous and so stable you'll be able to hold the bowl upside down and it won't run out. Use it in one of the following ways:

- On top of cold milk for Greek-style frappé

- On top of hot milk for a dalgona coffee

- Spooned over good vanilla ice cream, with a shot of Metaxa and a crisp, thin biscuit, for a fabulous pudding

A fancy coffee mousse

For something so astonishingly easy, this is a very chic pudding. Make it in the morning, and keep it in the fridge for a fairly effortless, entirely impressive dinner party finale.

SERVES 4

As above, plus
150ml double cream
1 tablespoon caster sugar
½ teaspoon vanilla extract

Make the frappé crema as above. In a separate bowl, whip the cream with the tablespoon of caster sugar until you have soft peaks. Fold in the vanilla, then fold through the coffee mousse. Spoon in soft folds into serving glasses and chill until needed.

V

Oregano, lemon and honey tea

Wild herb or mountain herb tea is a common drink in Greece, but getting hold of the right leaves does involve hunting down suppliers (which I've done for you on page 268). If that's not for you, create a similar flavour with fresh oregano, more readily available in larger supermarkets. I'd even go as far as suggesting you grow it yourself. I say that as someone who isn't terribly consistent in the garden, but it's a resilient plant and I've managed to keep all mine alive. They're much used, much loved and, in the long run, much cheaper.

MAKES 1 MUG

2 sprigs of oregano
2 tablespoons honey
1 slice of lemon

Place the oregano sprigs in your mug and top with just-boiled water. Leave to infuse for 5 minutes, then stir in the honey and pop in a slice of lemon.

V + GF

Mastiharita

The love child of a few of my favourite things: margaritas, mastiha, and basil in cocktails. Make the sugar syrup right now and store in a sterilised bottle, or in a jar in the fridge, so you can whip it out whenever you are in need of an instant, chic cocktail.

MAKES 1

50ml tequila
25ml mastiha
2–3 tablespoons basil syrup
 (below)
1 lemon
Ice cubes

Basil syrup (enough for LOTS of
 cocktails)
100g caster sugar
1 lemon
½ bunch of basil

For the basil syrup, place the caster sugar in a small saucepan with 100ml of water. Peel and add the zest of the lemon, in thick strips. Pop on a medium heat and bring to the boil, tear in the basil, and push it under the hot syrup. Immediately remove from the heat and leave to infuse for 15 minutes, then strain and cool the syrup, and chill until needed.

When you are ready to make your mastiharita, pour the tequila, mastiha, two to three tablespoons of the basil syrup (depending on how sweet you like your drinks) and the juice of half the lemon into a cocktail shaker. Add a handful of ice cubes and shake for 30 seconds. Have a taste and add some more lemon juice, if you like. Strain into a small glass and serve. I like mine straight up, but serve on the rocks, if you prefer.

VG + GF

Menus

My favourite Sunday lunch

• Pork shoulder, beans and chard
(page 171)

• Mum's sliced potatoes
(page 197)

• Roasted beets with caramelised nuts
(page 200)

• Herby skordalia
(page 79)

• Fried and pickled peppers
(page 202)

• Baklava cheesecake
(page 250)

Mezedes

• Fried sesame cheese bites
(page 67)

• Spiced honey calamari
(page 58)

• Spanakopita fritters
(page 100)

• Riganada tart with anchovies
(page 56)

• Beetroot and dill tzatziki with fried capers
(page 74)

• Patates antinahtes
(page 194)

• Addictive wings
(page 112)

• Strawberry and rose Cretan mess
(page 226)

• Cucumber and thyme lemonáda
(page 256)

Easy but fancy

• Sticky honey prawns
(page 102)

• Spiced lamb chops with houmous
(page 131)

• Roasted lemon, oregano and feta potatoes
(page 192)

• Cabbage, green bean and sesame salad
(page 198)

• A fancy coffee mousse
(page 259)

Going green — a plant-based feast

- Ladenia smash
(page 22)

- Chickpea and herb keftedes
(page 54)

- Artichoke houmous
(page 78)

- Sticky aubergine, pomegranate and herb tart
(page 91)

- Whole roast cabbage
(page 154)

- Crispy rice, pomegranate and herb salad
(page 208)

- Charred green beans, asparagus and almonds
(page 203)

- Wine-poached nectarines
(page 231)

A romantic night in

- Mastiharita
(page 262)

- Filo-wrapped feta with spiced honey
(page 64)

- Sole bourdeto with new potatoes
(page 106)

- Honeymoon salad (halve the recipe)
(page 205)

- Metaxa 'n' raisin ice cream
(page 237)

Do-ahead dinner party

- Figs and dates with anari and rosemary
(page 71)

- Youvetsi
(page 175)

- Dilly leeks and peas
(page 210)

- Sticky date and tahini aubergine
(page 189)

- Baklava ricotta semifreddo
(page 247)

Stockists

Ingredients, equipment, all your Mediterranean recipe needs

Agora Greek Delicacies
agoragreekdelicacies.co.uk

Bakalikon
bakalikon.co.uk

Cypressa
cypressa.co.uk

Cyprus BBQ
cyprusbbq.co.uk

Deli on the Green
020 8882 5631

Despina
despina-foods.co.uk

Hellenic Grocery
hellenicgrocery.co.uk

Maltby & Greek
maltbyandgreek.com

Odysea
odysea.com

Rooted Spices
rootedspices.com

Sous Chef
souschef.co.uk

Yasar Halim
yasarhalim.com

A glossary, and some tips on how to cook from this book

Making sure ingredients are accessible and recipes are clear is one of my biggest focuses as a recipe writer, but I also want to empower you with the confidence to cook intuitively. So here are a few explanations about ingredients and cooking insights that will help you get the most out of this book, or any of my recipes for that matter — and start to make them your own.

Ingredients

Aleppo pepper:
If there is a recipe that I want to add a little heat to, I tend to use either fresh chillies or Aleppo pepper. Aleppo pepper, sometimes sold as pul biber, is a vibrant red, dried chilli flake from Syria and Turkey, and is worth hunting down. It isn't the spiciest, but it has a well-rounded, slow-releasing heat and sweetness. If you use a regular dried red chilli flake instead, then start by using half the amount stated for Aleppo pepper, as it tends to be a little hotter.

Aubergines:
I always remove some of the skin if I am slicing and roasting or frying aubergine. My yiayia taught me to peel it off in strips, as the skin can be hard to digest. The only time I don't do this is if I am roasting it whole or in halves, so that it keeps its shape.

Chicken, spatchcocked:
For the chicken gyro on page 168 you will need to spatchcock your chicken first. If you can, ask your butcher to do this for you — it is a matter of seconds for them. If you have to do it yourself, it's very simple. Place your chicken, breast-side down, on a large chopping board, with the legs towards you. Use a pair of poultry scissors (or large, sturdy kitchen scissors), and cut up along each side of the parson's nose and backbone, cutting through the ribs as you go. Remove the backbone (you can keep it for stock, if you like). Turn the chicken over and flatten it out. Place the heel of your hand on the chicken and press down, flattening the breastbone. You will hear it break, and the chicken will lay flat.

Chicken, wings:
For the addictive chicken wings on page 112, it's best to separate the wings into drumettes and flats. As with the spatchcocked chicken, you can ask your butcher to do this for you. However, if you buy your wings prepackaged, they often come in one piece. You can do it yourself by carefully cutting off the wing tip (save for stock) and then carefully chopping each wing down the main joint and breaking it into two.

Eggs:
The eggs I use are always large; this is particularly important when it comes to baking. And ideally free-range.

Filo and kataifi:
There are a few products where the supermarkets just do not always come up trumps. And one of those is pastry. The filo you get in most supermarket fridges is often not fit for purpose for a lot of the bakes in this book. The sheets are dry! And thick! You want those gorgeous, thin, almost transparent sheets. Some of the larger supermarkets have them in the freezer, and most international supermarkets or large grocers will have a good selection. Otherwise there is a list of suppliers at the back of this book. Hunt the good stuff down if you can, buy in bulk and store in the freezer until needed. And the same goes for kataifi; I always buy several packs as they last for ages.

Halloumi:
My Queen of All Cheese. You can get very good Cypriot halloumi in the supermarkets now. Actually, if it is called halloumi, you know that it has been made in Cyprus, and will be made with goat's or sheep's milk, or a mixture. If you find halloumi-style cheese made with cow's milk, just pass by.

Herbs:
If you can, try to hunt down fresh herbs from an international grocery shop or good local grocer. They are less likely to be packed in unnecessary plastic, and have an impressive amount of flavour. However, supermarket herbs are still often good, and I know that many people, including me, buy them. So, when I talk about bunches of herbs in this book, I am referring to supermarket bunches, generally 20–30g in weight.

Mastiha:

One of my favourite spirits, made with mastic (a resin from trees on the island of Chios). It is sweet, and has a woody, evergreen, pine-y flavour, and is very, very delicious. It's gorgeous chilled and sipped after a meal, a bit like limoncello. I also like to mix it up, perhaps in the drinks at the end of this book.

Mussels:

To make sure mussels are safe for eating you want to give them a good clean in fresh cold water. Remove any beards or stringy bits. If the mussels are open, tap them gently at the opening with the side of a table knife. If they are OK to eat, they will close. If they are dead, they will remain open. You want to chuck these.

Oil:

For me, oil is always olive oil. I use the light, milder variety for frying and save the good, peppery, extra virgin stuff for finishing dishes. It's only if I am deep-frying that I will use a neutral, flavourless oil such as vegetable, sunflower or groundnut.

Orange blossom water and rose water:

A lot of people claim to not love flower waters, but I think that is because they are used with a heavy hand, so taste like perfume. If you are nervous, add a little and taste as you go. Be wary of over-concentrated extracts and essences based on alcohol and oils. Both orange flower and rose water should come in a large bottle, and you never need more than one or two tablespoons.

Pomegranate molasses:

Made from the boiled-down juice of sour pomegranates, this thick, deep red syrup is wonderfully sweet and sour. Often used in marinades or for finishing dishes.

Seasoning:

Unless stated, salt in this book is always flaky sea salt (I love Maldon or Cornish Sea Salt Co). In baking I will always use, and specify, fine sea salt, so that it is easily distributed in the bake. Be mindful that if there is a recipe with a volume measure of salt, these two different types of salt will equate to very different weights. Black pepper should ideally be freshly ground, to give you the best flavour.

Stock:

I am not a snob and do not judge when it comes to stock. Sure, if you have the time to make your own, then of course it will be incredible. But we aren't all chefs who spend all day in a kitchen, or even all day at home. Buying tubs of ready-made stock is a good shout if you can, but they are often way more expensive than buying it in cube form. (And honestly, not all ready-made stock is equal.) I want my recipes to appeal to everyone, so if you have a stock cube, please use it. I do. All these recipes were tested using them.

Tahini:

Thankfully tahini has become quite easy to find and you'll often find a variety of brands in larger supermarkets. It's a paste made from ground sesame seeds. Make sure to always give it a good stir before using as the oil will often sit on the top of the jar.

Equipment and guides

Measurements:

I use electric scales and UK spoon measures — 15ml tablespoons and 5ml teaspoons. Unless instructed, spoon measures are always level, never heaped.

Oven:

All the recipes were developed and tested in a fan-assisted oven. I've given the equivalent temperature settings for conventional and gas ovens, too. (Many recipes have also been tested in conventional and gas ovens.) It's worth getting familiar with how your oven cooks, especially for baking. If it seems unpredictable, then consider investing in an oven thermometer. They are relatively inexpensive and sit or hang happily in the oven so you know the precise temperature.

Substitutions and dietary requirements:

Throughout this book, I have marked recipes that are suitable for or can be adapted to various diets: vegetarian, vegan, gluten-free and dairy-free. If I've made a suggested substitution, it's because I've tested it. If you're a confident cook, you may be able to make further adaptations.

Index

A

addictive wings 112

afternoon chamomile and honey cake 218

Aleppo pepper 270

almonds: afternoon chamomile and honey cake 218

charred green beans, asparagus and almonds 203

anari 62

figs and dates with anari and rosemary 71

village pasta with chicken and lemon 117

anchovies: honeymoon tomatoes, avocado and anchovies 205

riganada tart with anchovies 56

anise, wine-poached nectarines with 231

apricot jam: the HLT v the HMT 26

apricots: apricot and honey sorbet 240

apricot and orange blossom mess 228

whole grilled halloumi with apricots 68

artichoke houmous 78

asparagus: charred green beans, asparagus and almonds 203

aubergines 270

hasselback imam bayildi 150

roasted aubergine, tomato, garlic and feta pasta 88

sizzling melitzanosalata 75

sticky aubergine, pomegranate and herb tart 91

sticky date and tahini aubergine 189

avocados: honeymoon tomatoes, avocado and anchovies 205

tuna, egg and caper salad 110

B

bacon: HLT kritharaki 120

baklava, a love story and inspiration 242

baklava buns 244

baklava cake 249

baklava cheesecake, I love you 250-3

baklava ricotta semifreddo 247

Holly's baklava French toast 40

barbecued sea bass stuffed with pistachio and caper pesto 109

basil syrup: mastiharita 262

beans: pork shoulder, beans and chard 171

village sausages, beans and peppers on toast 31

beef: classic biftekia and chips 126

little meat pies 178

meatballs in chilli tomatoes with eggs 32

my favourite meat and orzo stew 175

one-pan pastitsio 124

spiced beef with pasta 176

beer with a side of battered gigantes 60

beetroot: beetroot and dill tzatziki with fried capers 74

roasted beets with caramelised nuts 200

biftekia: classic biftekia and chips 126

bobota 25

bougatsa, praline 42

bourdeto: sole bourdeto with new potatoes 106

bread: cheesy green chilli cornbread 25

everyday yoghurt flatbreads 34-9

the HLT v the HMT 26

tomato, onion and oregano toast 22

village sausages, beans and peppers on toast 31

see also brioche; pita breads

breakfast soutzoukakia 32

bream, lemon and herb salt-baked 160

brioche: Holly's baklava French toast 40

brittle: pasteli yoghurt 50

bulgur wheat: roast chicken with tomatoey bulgur wheat 166

simple pilafi 211

buns: baklava buns 244

pillowy chestnut knots 47-9

butter: burnt butter eggs and goat's cheese 20

corn on the cob with thyme and burnt butter 207

salted honey butter flatbreads 39

whipped feta with brown butter pine nut flatbreads 38

whole roast cabbage with spiced butter 154

butter beans: a beer with a side of battered gigantes 60

caramelised onion, leek and courgette butter beans 152

pork shoulder, beans and chard 171

butternut squash: pumpkin and feta kataifi pie 157

roasted squash, kataifi and pomegranate salad 212

C

cabbage: cabbage, green bean and sesame salad 198

charred cabbage, lemon and rice soup 84

chopped kebab salad 146

whole roast cabbage with spiced butter 154

cakes: afternoon chamomile and honey cake 218

baklava cake 249

chocolate party cake 216

Greek coffee-walnut layer cake 221

calamari, spiced honey 58

capers: baked fish with tomatoes and olives 158

barbecued sea bass stuffed with pistachio and caper pesto 109

beetroot and dill tzatziki with fried capers 74

caper mayo 139

tuna, egg and caper salad 110

caramelised onion, leek and courgette butter beans 152

cardamom pods: golden filo custard pie 222

carrots: golden fish soup 163
    my favourite meat and orzo stew 175
    spiced beef with pasta 176

cauliflower: crispy cauliflower and lentils with herby green olive dressing 190

chamomile tea: afternoon chamomile and honey cake 218

chard, pork shoulder, beans and 171

charred cabbage, lemon and rice soup 84

charred green beans, asparagus and almonds 203

charred oyster mushrooms, mustard and thyme 134

charred pepper and olive strapatsada 28

cheese 62, 271
    addictive wings 112
    baklava cheesecake, I love you 250-3
    burnt butter eggs and goat's cheese 20
    cheesy green chilli cornbread 25
    feta, cherry and white chocolate cookies 232
    figs and dates with anari and rosemary 71
    filo-wrapped feta with spiced honey 64
    fried sesame cheese bites 67
    grilled watermelon breakfast salad 45
    hasselback imam bayildi 150
    a jar of marinated feta 72
    lemon and oregano chicken with a feta dip, two ways 112
    one-pan pastitsio 124
    one-pot chicken thighs and rice 114
    prawn saganaki kebabs 138
    pumpkin and feta kataifi pie 157
    roasted aubergine, tomato, garlic and feta pasta 88
    roasted lemon, oregano and feta potatoes 192
    roasted squash, kataifi and pomegranate salad 212
    spanakopita fritters 100

spanakopita jacket potatoes 96
spanakorisotto 99
watermelon, feta and cucumber 186
whipped feta with brown butter pine nut flatbreads 38
see also halloumi

cheesecake, baklava 250-3

cherries: feta, cherry and white chocolate cookies 232

chestnut purée: pillowy chestnut knots 47-9

chicken 270-1
    addictive wings 112
    halloumi fried chicken 118
    lemon and oregano chicken with a feta dip, two ways 112
    one-pot chicken thighs and rice 114
    pulled chicken gyro with all the trimmings 168
    roast chicken, potatoes and peppers 165
    roast chicken with tomatoey bulgur wheat 166
    spiced chilli and coriander chicken 142
    village pasta with chicken and lemon 117

chickpeas: artichoke houmous 78
    chickpea and herb keftedes 54
    little lamb meatballs with chickpeas 128

chillies: cheesy green chilli cornbread 25
    meatballs in chilli tomatoes with eggs 32
    spiced chilli and coriander chicken 142

chips: classic biftekia and chips 126
    crispy garlic oven chips 146
    everything pita chips 80

chocolate: baklava cheesecake 250-3
    chocolate hazelnut custard filo pie 42
    chocolate party cake 216
    feta, cherry and white chocolate cookies 232

chocolate spread: tahini, date and chocolate spread flatbreads 39

chopped kebab salad 146

cinnamon: chilled cinnamon and rose rice pudding 254

coffee: a fancy coffee mousse 259
    frappé crema 259
    Greek coffee-walnut layer cake 221

cookies, feta, cherry and white chocolate 232

coriander: cabbage, green bean and sesame salad 198
    pan-fried new potatoes with red wine and coriander 194
    spiced chilli and coriander chicken 142

corn on the cob with thyme and burnt butter 207

cornbread, cheesy green chilli 25

courgettes: caramelised onion, leek and courgette butter beans 152
    spanakopita fritters 100

cream: apricot and orange blossom mess 228
    baklava cheesecake 250-3
    baklava ricotta semifreddo 247
    chilled cinnamon and rose rice pudding 254
    ekmek pie 234
    a fancy coffee mousse 259
    golden filo custard pie 222
    Greek coffee-walnut layer cake 221
    Metaxa 'n' raisin ice cream 237
    olive oil ice cream slice 238
    pumpkin and feta kataifi pie 157
    rose and strawberry Cretan mess 226

cream cheese: baklava cheesecake, I love you 250-3
    tahini cream cheese frosting 244

crème fraîche: one-pan pastitsio 124

Cretan mess, rose and strawberry 226

crispy cauliflower and lentils with herby green olive dressing 190

crispy garlic oven chips 146

crispy rice, pomegranate and herb salad 208

cucumber: beetroot and dill tzatziki with fried capers 74
    chopped kebab salad 146
    cucumber and thyme lemonáda 256
    the HLT v the HMT 26
    watermelon, feta and cucumber 186

custard: golden filo custard pie 222

D

dates: figs and dates with anari and
   rosemary 71
   sticky date and tahini aubergine 189
   tahini, date and chocolate spread
      flatbreads 39
dill: beetroot and dill tzatziki with fried
   capers 74
   dilly leeks and peas 210
dips: herby skordalia 79
   sizzling melitzanosalata 75
dressing, herby green olive 190
drinks: cucumber and thyme
   lemonáda 256
   frappé crema 259
   ginger lemonade 255
   mastiharita 262
   oregano, lemon and honey tea 260
dukkah: pumpkin and feta kataifi pie 157

E

eggs 271
   burnt butter eggs and goat's cheese 20
   charred pepper and olive
      strapatsada 28
   ekmek pie 234
   Holly's baklava French toast 40
   lamb shank fricassee with preserved
      lemon 180
   meatballs in chilli tomatoes with
      eggs 32
   meringues 225
   tuna, egg and caper salad 110
ekmek pie 234
endives: lamb shank fricassee with
   preserved lemon 180
equipment 273
Eton mess 224, 226
everyday yoghurt flatbreads 34–9
everything pita chips 80

F

fennel: braised sausage, lentils and
   fennel 123
   lemon and herb salt-baked bream 160
   saffron and fennel fish kebabs with
      caper mayo 139
   triple-fennel pork belly 172
fennel seeds: lemon and herb salt-baked
   bream 160
   triple-fennel pork belly 172
feta 62
   addictive wings 112
   baklava cheesecake 250–3
   cheesy green chilli cornbread 25
   feta, cherry and white chocolate
      cookies 232
   filo-wrapped feta with spiced
      honey 64
   grilled watermelon breakfast salad 45
   hasselback imam bayildi 150
   a jar of marinated feta 72
   lemon and oregano chicken with a
      feta dip, two ways 112
   one-pot chicken thighs and rice 114
   prawn saganaki kebabs 138
   pumpkin and feta kataifi pie 157
   roasted aubergine, tomato, garlic and
      feta pasta 88
   roasted lemon, oregano and feta
      potatoes 192
   roasted squash, kataifi and pome-
      granate salad 212
   spanakopita fritters 100
   spanakopita jacket potatoes 96
   spanakorisotto 99
   watermelon, feta and cucumber 186
   whipped feta with brown butter pine
      nut flatbreads 38
figs and dates with anari and
   rosemary 71
filo pastry 271
   baklava cheesecake, I love you 250–3
   baklava ricotta semifreddo 247
   chocolate hazelnut custard filo pie 42
   filo-wrapped feta with spiced
      honey 64
   golden filo custard pie 222
   little meat pies 178
fish: baked fish with tomatoes and
   olives 158
   barbecued sea bass stuffed with
      pistachio and caper pesto 109
   golden fish soup 163
   honeymoon tomatoes, avocado and
      anchovies 205
   lemon and herb salt-baked bream 160
   riganada tart with anchovies 56
   saffron and fennel fish kebabs with
      caper mayo 139
   sole bourdeto with new potatoes 106
   tuna, egg and caper salad 110
flatbreads: everyday yoghurt
   flatbreads 34–9
   pulled chicken gyro with all the
      trimmings 168
   salted honey butter flatbreads 39
   tahini, date and chocolate spread
      flatbreads 39
   whipped feta with brown butter pine
      nut flatbreads 38
frappé crema 259
French toast, baklava 40
fricassee: lamb shank fricassee with
   preserved lemon 180
fritters, spanakopita 100
frosting, tahini cream cheese 244

G

gala trin 46
galatopita 222
garlic: beetroot and dill tzatziki with
   fried capers 74
   crispy garlic oven chips 146
   herby skordalia 79
   pork shoulder, beans and chard 171
   roast chicken, potatoes and
      peppers 165
   roasted aubergine, tomato, garlic and
      feta pasta 88
   roasted lemon, oregano and feta
      potatoes 192
   slow-roasted 30 garlic lamb
      shoulder 183
   tomato, onion and oregano toast 22
   triple-fennel pork belly 172
gigantes: a beer with a side of battered
   gigantes 60
   green gigantes 152
ginger lemonade 255
goat's cheese, burnt butter eggs and 20
golden filo custard pie 222
golden fish soup 163
golden mustard sauce 146

graviera 62
  fried sesame cheese bites 67
  one-pan pastitsio 124
  spanakopita jacket potatoes 96
Greek coffee-walnut layer cake 221
green beans: cabbage, green bean and
  sesame salad 198
  charred green beans, asparagus and
    almonds 203
green gigantes 152
gyro, pulled chicken 168

H

halloumi 62, 271
  halloumi fried chicken 118
  halloumi, tomato and honey
    kebabs 135
  HLT kritharaki 120
  the HLT v the HMT 26
  lamb and halloumi kofta 144
  my favourite meat and orzo stew 175
  understated lentils with halloumi 86
  village pasta with chicken and
    lemon 117
  whole grilled halloumi with
    apricots 68
hasselback imam bayildi 150
hazelnuts: chocolate hazelnut custard
  filo pie 42
herbs 271
  chickpea and herb keftedes 54
  crispy rice, pomegranate and herb
    salad 208
  herby green olive dressing 190
  herby skordalia 79
  lemon and herb salt-baked bream 160
  sticky aubergine, pomegranate and
    herb tart 91
hilopites, mushroom and lentil 92
HLT kritharaki 120
the HLT v the HMT 26
Holly's baklava French toast 40
honey: afternoon chamomile and honey
  cake 218
  apricot and honey sorbet 240
  apricot and orange blossom
    mess 228
  baklava cake 249

baklava cheesecake 250–3
baklava ricotta semifreddo 247
figs and dates with anari and
  rosemary 71
filo-wrapped feta with spiced
  honey 64
fried sesame cheese bites 67
halloumi, tomato and honey
  kebabs 135
Holly's baklava French toast 40
oregano, lemon and honey tea 260
pasteli yoghurt 50
pumpkin and feta kataifi pie 157
rose and strawberry Cretan mess 226
salted honey butter flatbreads 39
spiced honey calamari 58
sticky honey prawns 102
whole grilled halloumi with
  apricots 68
honeymoon tomatoes, avocado and
  anchovies 205
houmous: artichoke houmous 78
  spiced lamb chops with houmous 131

I

ice cream: baklava ricotta
  semifreddo 247
  Metaxa 'n' raisin ice cream 237
  olive oil ice cream slice 238
imam bayildi, hasselback 150

J

jacket potatoes, spanakopita 96

K

karydopita 221
kataifi pastry 271
  ekmek pie 234
  pumpkin and feta kataifi pie 157
  roasted squash, kataifi and pome-
    granate salad 212
kebabs: charred oyster mushrooms,
  mustard and thyme 134
  halloumi, tomato and honey
    kebabs 135
  prawn saganaki kebabs 138

saffron and fennel fish kebabs with
  caper mayo 139
kefalograviera 62
kefalotyri 62
  addictive wings 112
  figs and dates with anari and
    rosemary 71
  fried sesame cheese bites 67
  one-pot chicken thighs and rice 114
  spanakorisotto 99
keftedes, chickpea and herb 54
kofta, lamb and halloumi 144
kreatopites 178
kritharaki, HLT 120

L

ladenia smash 22
lamb: lamb and halloumi kofta 144
  lamb shank fricassee with preserved
    lemon 180
  little lamb meatballs with
    chickpeas 128
  little meat pies 178
  my favourite meat and orzo stew 175
  slow-roasted 30 garlic lamb
    shoulder 183
  spiced lamb chops with houmous 131
leeks: caramelised onion, leek and
  courgette butter beans 152
  dilly leeks and peas 210
  golden fish soup 163
  little meat pies 178
  spanakorisotto 99
lemon sole bourdeto with new
  potatoes 106
lemonade: cucumber and thyme
  lemonáda 256
  ginger lemonade 255
lemons: addictive wings 112
  cabbage, green bean and sesame
    salad 198
  charred cabbage, lemon and rice
    soup 84
  cucumber and thyme lemonáda 256
  ginger lemonade 255
  golden fish soup 163
  lamb shank fricassee with preserved
    lemon 180

lemon and herb salt-baked bream 160

lemon and oregano chicken with a
feta dip, two ways 112

mastiharita 262

one-pot chicken thighs and rice 114

oregano, lemon and honey tea 260

pulled chicken gyro with all the
trimmings 168

roasted lemon, oregano and feta
potatoes 192

village pasta with chicken and
lemon 117

lentils: braised sausage, lentils and
fennel 123

crispy cauliflower and lentils with
herby green olive dressing 190

mushroom and lentil hilopites 92

understated lentils with halloumi 86

lettuce: lamb shank fricassee with
preserved lemon 180

little lamb meatballs with chickpeas 128

little meat pies 178

loukoumi 226

lountza: HLT kritharaki 120

the HLT v the HMT 26

M

manouri 62

marmalade: olive oil ice cream slice 238

mastiha 272

mastiharita 262

mayonnaise: addictive wings 112

caper mayo 139

golden mustard sauce 146

the HLT v the HMT 26

one-pot chicken thighs and rice 114

meatballs: little lamb meatballs with
chickpeas 128

meatballs in chilli tomatoes with
eggs 32

melitzanosalata, sizzling 75

menus 266-7

meringues 225

apricot and orange blossom mess 228

rose and strawberry Cretan mess 226

Metaxa 'n' raisin ice cream 237

milk: chilled cinnamon and rose rice
pudding 254

chocolate hazelnut custard filo pie 42

ekmek pie 234

pumpkin and feta kataifi pie 157

spiced milk and pasta 46

Mum's sliced potatoes 197

mushrooms: charred oyster mushrooms, mustard and thyme 134

mushroom and lentil hilopites 92

mussels 272

mussels in saffron yoghurt 105

mustard: charred oyster mushrooms,
mustard and thyme 134

golden mustard sauce 146

my favourite meat and orzo stew 175

N

nectarines, wine-poached 231

noodles: one-pot chicken thighs and
rice 114

simple pilafi 211

understated lentils with halloumi 86

nuts: baklava cake 249

pasteli yoghurt 50

roasted beets with caramelised
nuts 200

O

oil 272

olive oil ice cream slice 238

olives: baked fish with tomatoes and
olives 158

charred pepper and olive
strapatsada 28

herby green olive dressing 190

roast chicken, potatoes and
peppers 165

triple-fennel pork belly 172

one-pan pastitsio 124

one-pot chicken thighs and rice 114

onions: caramelised onion, leek and
courgette butter beans 152

slow-roasted 30 garlic lamb
shoulder 183

tomato, onion and oregano toast 22

understated lentils with halloumi 86

orange blossom water 272

apricot and orange blossom mess 228

ekmek pie 234

Holly's baklava French toast 40

oranges: baklava buns 244

baklava cake 249

oregano: classic pork with oregano 143

lemon and oregano chicken with a
feta dip, two ways 112

oregano, lemon and honey tea 260

roasted lemon, oregano and feta
potatoes 192

tomato, onion and oregano toast 22

orzo: HLT kritharaki 120

my favourite meat and orzo stew 175

P

pasta: HLT kritharaki 120

mushroom and lentil hilopites 92

my favourite meat and orzo stew 175

one-pan pastitsio 124

roasted aubergine, tomato, garlic and
feta pasta 88

spiced beef with pasta 176

spiced milk and pasta 46

understated lentils with halloumi 86

village pasta with chicken and
lemon 117

pasteli yoghurt 50

pastitsada 176

pastitsio, one-pan 124

patates antinahtes 194

peas, dilly leeks and 210

peppers: charred pepper and olive
strapatsada 28

fried and pickled peppers 202

roast chicken, potatoes and
peppers 165

village sausages, beans and peppers
on toast 31

pesto, barbecued sea bass stuffed with
pistachio and caper 109

pies: chocolate hazelnut custard filo
pie 42

ekmek pie 234

golden filo custard pie 222

little meat pies 178

pumpkin and feta kataifi pie 157

pilafi, simple 211

pillowy chestnut knots 47-9

pine nuts: whipped feta with brown
  butter pine nut flatbreads 38
pistachios: barbecued sea bass stuffed
  with pistachio and caper pesto 109
  ekmek pie 234
  grilled watermelon breakfast salad 45
pita chips, everything 80
politiki kouzina 150
pomegranate: crispy rice, pomegranate
  and herb salad 208
  roasted squash, kataifi and pomegranate salad 212
  sticky aubergine, pomegranate and
  herb tart 91
pomegranate molasses 272
pork: classic pork with oregano 143
  little meat pies 178
  my favourite meat and orzo stew 175
  pork shoulder, beans and chard 171
  triple-fennel pork belly 172
potatoes: chickpea and herb keftedes 54
  classic biftekia and chips 126
  crispy garlic oven chips 146
  golden fish soup 163
  herby skordalia 79
  Mum's sliced potatoes 197
  pan-fried new potatoes with red wine
  and coriander 194
  patates antinahtes 194
  roast chicken, potatoes and
  peppers 165
  roasted lemon, oregano and feta
  potatoes 192
  sole bourdeto with new potatoes 106
  spanakopita jacket potatoes 96
  tuna, egg and caper salad 110
praline bougatsa 42
prawns: prawn saganaki kebabs 138
  sticky honey prawns 102
preserved lemon, lamb shank fricassee
  with 180
psari plaki 158
psarosoupa 163
puff pastry: riganada tart with
  anchovies 56
  sticky aubergine, pomegranate and
  herb tart 91
pulled chicken gyro with all the
  trimmings 168

pumpkin and feta kataifi pie 157
pumpkin seeds: pasteli yoghurt 50

R

ragu: one-pan pastitsio 124
raisins: Metaxa 'n' raisin ice cream 237
rice: charred cabbage, lemon and rice
  soup 84
  chilled cinnamon and rose rice
  pudding 254
  crispy rice, pomegranate and herb
  salad 208
  one-pot chicken thighs and rice 114
  spanakorisotto 99
ricotta: baklava ricotta semifreddo 247
  figs and dates with anari and
  rosemary 71
riganada tart with anchovies 56
rizogalo 254
rose loukoumi: rose and strawberry
  Cretan mess 226
rose water 272
  baklava cheesecake 250-3
  chilled cinnamon and rose rice
  pudding 254
rosemary, figs and dates with anari
  and 71

S

saffron: mussels in saffron yoghurt 105
  saffron and fennel fish kebabs with
  caper mayo 139
saganaki kebabs, prawn 138
salads 184-213
  cabbage, green bean and sesame
  salad 198
  chopped kebab salad 146
  crispy cauliflower and lentils with
  herby green olive dressing 190
  crispy rice, pomegranate and herb
  salad 208
  grilled watermelon breakfast salad 45
  honeymoon tomatoes, avocado and
  anchovies 205
  roasted squash, kataifi and pomegranate salad 212
  sizzling melitzanosalata 75

sticky date and tahini aubergine 189
  tuna, egg and caper salad 110
  watermelon, feta and cucumber 186
salted honey butter flatbreads 39
sandwich: the HLT v the HMT 26
sausages: braised sausage, lentils and
  fennel 123
  village sausages, beans and peppers
  on toast 31
sea bass: barbecued sea bass stuffed
  with pistachio and caper pesto 109
seasoning 272
semifreddo, baklava ricotta 247
sesame seeds: cabbage, green bean and
  sesame salad 198
  everything pita chips 80
  fried sesame cheese bites 67
  grilled watermelon breakfast
  salad 45
  pasteli yoghurt 50
shellfish: golden fish soup 163
simple pilafi 211
sizzling melitzanosalata 75
skordalia, herby 79
skordostoumbi pasta 88
slow-roasted 30 garlic lamb
  shoulder 183
sokolatopita 216
sole bourdeto with new potatoes 106
sorbet, apricot and honey 240
soups: charred cabbage, lemon and rice
  soup 84
  golden fish soup 163
soutzoukakia, breakfast 32
spanakopita 94
spanakopita jacket potatoes 96
spanakopita fritters 100
spanakorisotto 99
spiced beef with pasta 176
spiced butter, whole roast cabbage
  with 154
spiced chilli and coriander chicken 142
spiced honey: filo-wrapped feta with
  spiced honey 64
  spiced honey calamari 58
spiced lamb chops with houmous 131
spiced milk and pasta 46
spinach: spanakopita fritters 100
  spanakopita jacket potatoes 96

spanakorisotto 99

spring onions: cheesy green chilli
cornbread 25
  crispy rice, pomegranate and herb
  salad 208
  lamb shank fricassee with preserved
  lemon 180
  spanakopita jacket potatoes 96

squash: pumpkin and feta kataifi pie 157
  roasted squash, kataifi and
  pomegranate salad 212

squid: spiced honey calamari 58

stew, my favourite meat and orzo 175

sticky aubergine, pomegranate and herb
tart 91

sticky date and tahini aubergine 189

sticky honey prawns 102

stock 273

strapatsada, charred pepper and
olive 28

strawberries: rose and strawberry
Cretan mess 226

Swiss chard: village pasta with chicken
and lemon 117

syrup, basil 262

T

tahini 273
  artichoke houmous 78
  sizzling melitzanosalata 75
  sticky date and tahini aubergine 189
  tahini cream cheese frosting 244
  tahini, date and chocolate spread
  flatbreads 39

tarts: riganada tart with anchovies 56
  sticky aubergine, pomegranate
  and herb tart 91

tea, oregano, lemon and honey 260

tequila: mastiharita 262

thyme: charred oyster mushrooms,
mustard and thyme 134
  corn on the cob with thyme and burnt
  butter 207
  cucumber and thyme lemonáda 256

toast: baklava French toast 40
  tomato, onion and oregano toast 22
  village sausages, beans and peppers
  on toast 31

tomatoes: baked fish with tomatoes and
olives 158
  cabbage, green bean and sesame
  salad 198
  charred pepper and olive
  strapatsada 28
  chopped kebab salad 146
  halloumi, tomato and honey
  kebabs 135
  hasselback imam bayildi 150
  HLT kritharaki 120
  the HLT v the HMT 26
  honeymoon tomatoes, avocado and
  anchovies 205
  meatballs in chilli tomatoes with
  eggs 32
  my favourite meat and orzo stew 175
  prawn saganaki kebabs 138
  riganada tart with anchovies 56
  roast chicken, potatoes and peppers
  165
  roast chicken with tomatoey bulgur
  wheat 166
  roasted aubergine, tomato, garlic and
  feta pasta 88
  spiced beef with pasta 176
  tomato, onion and oregano toast 22

triple-fennel pork belly 172

tserepa 165

tuna, egg and caper salad 110

tzatziki, beetroot and dill 74

U

understated lentils with halloumi 86

V

vermicelli: simple pilafi 211

village pasta with chicken and
lemon 117

village sausages, beans and peppers on
toast 31

W

walnuts: baklava buns 244
  baklava cheesecake 250–3
  baklava ricotta semifreddo 247

Greek coffee-walnut layer cake 221
Holly's baklava French toast 40
pasteli yoghurt 50

watermelon: grilled watermelon
breakfast salad 45
  watermelon, feta and cucumber 186

whipped feta with brown butter pine nut
flatbreads 38

white beans: village sausages, beans
and peppers on toast 31

whole roast cabbage with spiced
butter 154

wine: pan-fried new potatoes with
red wine and coriander 194
  wine-poached nectarines with
  anise 231

Y

yoghurt: addictive wings 112
  apricot and orange blossom
  mess 228
  beetroot and dill tzatziki with fried
  capers 74
  cheesy green chilli cornbread 25
  everyday yoghurt flatbreads 34–9
  golden mustard sauce 146
  grilled watermelon breakfast
  salad 45
  lemon and herb salt-baked
  bream 160
  Metaxa 'n' raisin ice cream 237
  mussels in saffron yoghurt 105
  one-pot chicken thighs and rice 114
  pasteli yoghurt 50
  pulled chicken gyro with all the
  trimmings 168
  roast chicken with tomatoey bulgur
  wheat 166
  roasted beets with caramelised
  nuts 200
  rose and strawberry Cretan
  mess 226
  spanakopita jacket potatoes 96
  sticky date and tahini aubergine 189

youvetsi 175

Conversion tables

WEIGHTS

Metric	Imperial
15g	½oz
20g	¾oz
30g	1oz
55g	2oz
85g	3oz
110g	4oz / ¼lb
140g	5oz
170g	6oz
200g	7oz
225g	8oz / ½lb
255g	9oz
285g	10oz
310g	11oz
340g	12oz / ¾lb
370g	13oz
400g	14oz
425g	15oz
450g	6oz / 1lb
1kg	2lb 4oz
1.5kg	3lb 5oz

LIQUIDS

Metric	Imperial
5ml	1 teaspoon
15ml	1 tablespoon or ½fl oz
30ml	2 tablespoons or 1fl oz
150ml	¼ pint or 5fl oz
290ml	½ pint or 10fl oz
425ml	¾ pint or 16fl oz
570ml	1 pint or 20fl oz
1 litre	1 ¾ pints
1.2 litres	2 pints

LENGTH

Metric	Imperial
5mm	¼ in
1cm	½in
2cm	¾in
2.5cm	1in
5cm	2in
10cm	4in
15cm	6in
20cm	8in
30cm	12in

USEFUL CONVERSIONS

1 tablespoon = 3 teaspoons

1 egg = 65–73g / approx 60ml / approx 2fl oz

OVEN TEMPERATURES

°C	°C fan	Gas mark	°F
110°C	90°C fan	Gas mark ¼	225°F
120°C	100°C fan	Gas mark ½	250°F
140°C	120°C fan	Gas mark 1	275°F
150°C	130°C fan	Gas mark 2	300°F
160°C	140°C fan	Gas mark 3	325°F
180°C	160°C fan	Gas mark 4	350°F
190°C	170°C fan	Gas mark 5	375°F
200°C	180°C fan	Gas mark 6	400°F
220°C	200°C fan	Gas mark 7	425°F
230°C	210°C fan	Gas mark 8	450°F
240°C	220°C fan	Gas mark 9	475°F

Thank you

To my village:

Holly O'Neill. Where would I, and this book, be without you? Thank you not only for your wisdom and editorial knowledge, but for also spending entire days in the kitchen with me geeking out about food and constantly striving for excellence. Oh, and for apricot margaritas. There is no one I'd rather dissect a dish with. Felicity Blunt, thank you for helping me get this book off the ground and being the best cheerleader! And to Vanessa Fogarty for helping it fly. I adore you both. Rowan Yapp, Lena Hall, Ellen Williams, Shunayna Vaghela and all the wonderful team at Bloomsbury, I am eternally grateful that I get to work with you all. Thank you for believing in me.

To the best team in town! Laura Edwards, you gave the book *life* with your amazing eye. I have never met anyone who makes taking incredible photographs look so effortless, even in pouring rain outside café windows! Tab Hawkins, my Greek sister from another mister, you make our shoot days such a joy and I love you so much. To Joss Herd and Hattie Arnold, the dreamiest duo. I'd happily dance around my kitchen with you both forever. More kitchen karaoke discos please. Anna Green, thank you for your patience and guidance; you always bring a book together so sympathetically. Thank you for putting up with me!

Huge thank yous must also go out to Hannah, Flo and Rosie from Curtis Brown and Eshara and Rose from Bloomsbury. Kathy Steer, Kate Guest and Victoria Denne: thank you for giving my words such care and attention. To Irene for coming to the penultimate shoot for a girl-gang glow-up. We loved it! And Kalliope for letting us stay in her beautiful home in Crete, a time that will remain with me forever.

To my crew:

There are many people who have given me a chance over the years, which means I can write these books and pop up on screens. Jamie Oliver, Gennaro Contaldo, Amanda Ross, Charlie Critchfield, Karen Barnes, Lucy Battersby, Allan Jenkins, Gareth Grundy, Rachel Platt, Simon Rimmer, Tim Lovejoy, Matt Tebbutt, Scott Anderson, James Bedwell and Michaela Bowles: I cannot thank you all enough.

To my pals:

For testing my recipes and for keeping me upright. Claire and Vince, Helen, Anna, Vish and Nicole, Sarah and Ewan, Carly and Crispin, Alex and Ed, Kofi and Ceri, Hannah, Rachel, Frances and Callum, Vicke and Ed, Matt and Valentine, Scott and Lucy, Bella and Matthias, Esub, Trish and Ads, James and Charley, Rhi, Lorrae and Davidoff, Iain and Sam: I think you're all great.

To my loves:

Mum and Dad, as always. There's no way I could live my life as I do without your support. I am insanely thankful for everything you do for us all. Lulu, my yiayia Martha, Lala, Cassie, Stephen and Nephele: you're the best family a girl could have. To the Hayden massive and Betty and Trevor for always rooting for me. Pete, for honing your tasting skills, having the best palate and always being necessarily honest. There's no one whose opinion I value more, in all aspects of life, than yours. And to my girls, Persephone and Elektra: you are my world. There is nothing I wouldn't do for you both. Except I won't make you a second dinner, so well done for (mostly) eating what I give you. You'll thank me when you're older, I promise. I love you. x

GEORGINA HAYDEN grew up above her grandparents' Greek Cypriot taverna in London. She writes for publications such as *Observer Food Monthly*, the *Telegraph*, *Delicious Magazine* and *Waitrose Food*, for which she won the Fortnum and Mason Best Cookery Writer Award in 2021. She has appeared on BBC Radio 4's *Woman's Hour*, Channel 4's *Sunday Brunch*, BBC One's *Saturday Kitchen*, and was a judge on Channel 4's *The Great Cookbook Challenge with Jamie Oliver*. Her first cookbook was *Stirring Slowly* (2016), followed by *Taverna* (2019) and *Sunday Times* bestseller *Nistisima* (2022), which won Best New Cookbook at the *Observer Food Monthly* Awards. She lives in London with her family.